EIGG

EIGG

Judy Urquhart

Photographs by Eric Ellington

CANONGATE

First published in 1987
by Canongate Publishing Limited
17 Jeffrey Street, Edinburgh

British Library Cataloguing in Publication Data
Urquhart, Judy
Eigg.
1. Eigg — Description and travel
I. Title
914.11'85   DA880.E4
ISBN 0-86241-149-1

Typeset by Buccleuch Printers, Hawick, Scotland
Printed by Butler and Tanner, Frome, Somerset, England

CONTENTS

Map of Eigg reproduced from a map of Arisaig and Lochaber by kind permission of
of John Bartholomew & Son Ltd.

EIGG

The island of Eigg lies seven miles out in the Atlantic off the west coast of Scotland. It is one of the most beautiful, fertile and wooded of the Western Isles, a view endorsed by the poet Hugh MacDiarmid who once said, 'If I have to choose among the Hebrides – and I find it desperately difficult to do so – I choose Eigg'. It is part of a group called the Small Isles, whose other members are Rhum, Muck and Canna, and acts as their headquarters. They, in turn, are sandwiched between Skye and Mull and help form the Inner Hebrides which, with the Outer Hebrides, make up the number of islands geology has segmented from the north western mainland.

The name, subject to numerous puns, in fact has nothing to do with eggs but comes from a Gaelic word meaning 'The Notch' and describes the deep divide that separates the massive Scurr rock from the rest of the island. This has been called 'the most memorable landmark in the Hebridean seas' and gives the island its distinctive shape which, when seen from a distance, has been likened to a crouching lion. The head is formed by the Scurr rock, the back comprises a plateau of heather moor dissected by a backbone of small lochans, and its rump an area of rocky hills. Dramatically steep cliffs make up the sides, and the green, productive coastal land can be said to be the paws and tail.

This varied topography creates a rich, natural science. Eigg is noted for its extraordinary geology and awesome rock formations but it also has few equals in the profusion and variety of the plants, mosses, ferns and fungi that grow, the marine animals that swim the seas and birds that wheel overhead. Two pairs of golden eagles breed on Eigg and there is a unique colony of shearwaters. The island has a temperate climate, which is shown by the way palm trees and eucalyptus flourish in the sheltered lodge gardens. It is generally mild and frost free with an average rainfall of sixty inches and an occasional heatwave when the beaches get too hot for comfort and the sea as blue as the Mediterranean.

The island's wild, unspoilt scenery is part of what draws about 4,000 tourists to visit Eigg every year and sustains the fluctuating, indigenous population. This numbers about sixty-five people, most of whom live at the north end of the island where they form a crofting community farming 1,500 acres exempt from the freehold of the estate. The 5,000 acres that make up the rest of Eigg are farmed by the estate, whose owner, Keith Schellenberg, lives for part of the year with his family in the Italianate lodge. This is situated at the south end at the widest point of the island which measures roughly three miles wide by five long.

Many of the islanders, besides maintaining their crofts, also fill part-time jobs as postman, ferryman and special constable. Others run the post office, tea-room and craft-shop, or make baskets and wooden furniture. Half of the population are now incomers. Many came as visitors, or to work on the estate, and stayed, beguiled by the peculiar fascination exerted by the islands in general and by Eigg in particular. The life, according to Hugh MacDiarmid, is not 'a cowardly shirking of the great issues of life, as if these were the peculiar property of the maelstroms of big-city life', but rather offers an alternative. It also acts as a corrective to the town's rush and noise, a renewal for what the poet Wilfred Scawen Blunt called 'that other death for which love strews no roses, Death of the altered soul, lost, perished, forever gone'.

To the indigenous islanders the idea of requiring a vent from life is alien. For them Eigg is home but you have to be born and brought up here to really understand what this means. They can never feel isolated when every person is a relation, every hillock familiar, and the country, changing seasons, and weather are part of themselves. As one said, 'To be surrounded by so much beauty, that is a great thing. You might have a poor standard of living but that does not matter, you are part of the nature of the country. Everything fits and has its part. There is a freshness about life.'

In spite of this attachment it cannot be denied that many people have left for a different life, and it is only recently that the population has stabilised. Life is still lived at a fundamental level. Gaining the essentials takes time and ingenuity, leaving little energy to crave luxuries and, anyway, washing machines are useless when there is no electricity. It is a hard existence but addictive. After a while, incomers are not sure how they would survive on the mainland. 'Sometimes you wonder if you are missing out, but then you have other things.' Those who make sporadic visits south to get 'a bit of culture' soon miss the island and return.

The visitor from the south who comes by train and, seventeen hours after leaving London, negotiates himself on to the pier at Eigg, may reflect that, in this time, he could have taken an aeroplane half way round the world to Hong Kong. But he would not have reached anywhere more lovely or, in a sense, more foreign. On Eigg you step back to a slower, more civilised existence, where every individual counts, where life is subjected to the whims of weather and personalities, giving it an uncertainty and excitement not experienced in computer-run countries. There is time to stop and talk and survey the shifting scene of light and cloud over the hills and seas of the Inner Hebrides. The island also has a mysteriousness intensified by an ancient history and folk-lore.

Eigg may be small and its people few, but every stone has a story and every proper islander a long family history. If all was to be told in full this book would be several times as long. The history of Eigg is, in part, a history of the whole of Scotland. It may not have stood in the main-stream of events but it has caught all the backwash and contributed not a little of its own. Prehistoric man settled Eigg as did the early Christians and Vikings. It provided a base from which the Lords of the Isles rose to power and later came under the aegis of the Clanranald chiefs and was caught up in their piratical clan wars. Men from Eigg supported the Jacobite cause. When it was suppressed, the Clanranalds, their power gone and fortune spent, sold Eigg. During the 19th century it was owned by a series of extraordinary industrial barons who lavished their money on the island. Today, modern life and taxation have produced a new approach to island-owning and living. Catholicism has remained the main faith; the people of Eigg never gave way to strict 19th-century Protestantism, with its hatred of superstition, thereby preserving their rich store of myth, legend and song. These live on and, combined with the history, magnificent scenery and natural life, make the island one of the more exceptional.

PREHISTORIC TIMES

The first men arrived on Eigg during the Stone Age, around 6500 BC, offshoots of a group of nomadic hunter-gathers of European extraction who had settled in caves near Oban. These men made excursions up the coast in pursuit of food and gradually colonised the islands, preferring them to the mainland because, it is thought, they contained fewer of the fiercer animals.

They found an island that is a comparative newcomer in the geological history of the Western Isles. The Outer Hebrides were the first to be established some one thousand million years ago. They were probably part of the inner skeleton of a country contemporary with the mainland. Sixty million years later, erupting volcanoes spilled a series of hot laval flows over the Hebrides which solidified into sheets of great Estuarine rock. As

these rocks cooled they contracted and their contortions, together with more geological grumblings, produced much land movement. One shift created gaps which were filled by the sea and, in this way, the Inner Hebrides were formed and became islands. Eigg and Rhum were joined together at this stage but a later earthquake separated the two. The land beneath the Western Isles and the mainland continued to boil and eruptions on Rhum, Skye and Ardnamurchan poured first a layer of basalt lava over Eigg and next one of pitchstone. These laval flows completed the geological strata of the island.

This still soft rocky sandwich was then attacked by the weather and sea which, over millions of years, ate away at its sides and surface. Erosion of the top, pitchstone laval layer produced what Sir Archibald Geikie proclaimed is 'one of the most impressive monuments of denudation to be

Laval rock columns above Kildonnan

found within the British Isles'; the massive mile-long Scurr ridge, a ship of black rock whose prow is the mighty Scurr rock. Its sides, during the slow cooling and contraction of the lava, have become a jumbled mass of ribbed columns and its surface resembles a gigantic cobbled pavement. The columns, which are similar to those found at Fingal's Cave in Staffa and to the Giant's Causeway in Ireland, rest, like some 'bridge based on wooden piles', on the remains of an ancient pine forest. The trees were a unique species called *Pinus Eiggensis*. Basalt lava rock covers most of the upland areas of Eigg. Erosion has cut this away into a series of monumental cliffs whose sides reveal the varied geological parentage of Eigg.

On the north-west side, friable sandstone and limestone rocks have broken from the main cliff face leaving narrow passageways and hidden waterfalls. Beyond, they have weathered into a series of weird arches, doorways and canopies. Round the north end the cliffs splinter into grey spires, their sheer sides scaly with slipping debris, while the sea's edge is littered with huge, red, coffin-shaped rocks making it look like some undertaker's backyard. Down the east coast layers of red sandstone, limestone and Jurassic shales jostle in magnificent confusion. In other places the corrosive effect of the sea on the friable rock has produced deep and lofty caves. The level of the sea has fallen, leaving raised beaches, and at the Singing Sands beach, *Camus Sgiotaig*, its wear has ground the rock into perfectly circular, fine quartz grains, each surrounded by minute pockets of air. When the sand is walked on or rubbed in dry weather it emits a long, squeaking, musical tone.

Ravages during the Ice Age finished the major structuring of the island. Glacial sheets creeping from the south-east made heavy scrapes, leaving crevasses which have been filled with water and become lochans, and moved enormous boulders, some the size of houses. There is one especially large and distinct rock at Grulin called *Cnoc Hosdail*. It is said to have been thrown by a giant on Muck at one on Eigg during a quarrel when, in anger, he ran out of words. How immensely strong this giant must have been to hurl this rock, which weighs one hundred tons, across two-and-a-half miles of sea. Some parts of the island are thought to have escaped the ice as, on the western Ben Buidhe cliffs and south-western moorlands, alpine plants grow which are not usually found in glaciated areas.

Around 10,000 BC the ice finally retreated and some time after the island was colonised by prehistoric reptiles. The 19th-century geologist Hugh Miller went 'hunting dead crocodiles' and found the shores of the north end 'fretted over' with the remains of fishes, bivalves, ammonites and bellamites and the remains of pliosaurus and pterodactyl. 'How strange,' he mused, 'that this sea should once have been thronged by reptile shapes more strange than poet ever imagined – dragons, gorgons and chimeras!' and most extraordinary of all reptiles, the pliosaurus. Here, this monstrous dragon, described as looking like 'a snake threaded through a tortoise', must have 'disported and fed; here they must have raised their little reptile heads and long swan-like necks over the surface to watch an antagonist or select a victim; here must they have warred and wedded and pursued all the various instincts of their unknown natures'.

These reptiles lived on in the myths of Eigg. The Massacre Cave, *Uamh Fhraing*, on the south coast, was believed to have been inhabited by a family of dragons or winged demons. It was told how, long, long ago, the dragons could be seen leaving the cave at dawn and returning at dusk and flying out to sea. They were terrible beyond words and their wings were so large they blotted out the sun. One day there was a great storm which must have been part of a war between the dragons and the sea-gods because it was like no ordinary storm. The next day the body of one of the dragons was found dead on the beach. It was of enormous size, far larger then any man, and had a terrible beak with teeth, and huge skin wings like a bat. After this only one dragon was seen coming and going at dawn and dusk. Later, it was no longer seen and, afraid but curious, the men of Eigg cautiously approached the cave. They were greeted by a stench so horrible they could go no further. The smell of dragons was known to be alarming but this was appalling. Never again did anyone approach the cave until the 6th century when St Donnan braved its

The Scurr ridge with its cobbled 'pavement' of laval rock

interior. He found the skeleton of 'the great flying dragon' on the cave floor, lying alone where he had died, a poor, forlorn and perhaps frightened creature.

Men had definitely settled Eigg by the late Stone Age judging from a flint arrowhead and some stone implements found near Kildonnan. They made a base here and, later, at Laig where, during the early Bronze Age, they buried their dead in stone cists often placing them in cairns. Here they cultivated the naturally fertile land with primitive implements and sheltered their fishing boats in the shallow bays. By 1600 BC these men were supplanted by others who knew about bronze but they left few traces apart from a socketed axe. Around 8000 BC a dark-haired Celtic people of ancient Indo-European stock, whose language forms the basis of Gaelic, pushed into Scotland to be followed, in 400 BC, by another influx known as the Brythonic Celts. They invaded Wales, Cornwall and Brittany, except for one branch who made their way into Scotland, probably via Ireland, and became known as the Picts. From 100 BC to 100 AD the Picts were attacked by further incoming tribes and, on Eigg, they built two defensive duns on rocky outcrops at the pier and Kildonnan the remains of which can still be traced.

The Picts also fortified two sites on the Scurr. A drystone wall, now nearly reduced to rubble, was built, barricading the top of the rock, inside which the people kept themselves warm with huge fires of peat moss – a fact deduced from finds of pumice-like stone converted from pitchstone fragments brought to a white heat by embers fanned by the frequent high winds. A second fort was created on an islet in the Lochan nam Ben Mora which lies just below the Scurr rock. Here, a small crannog was constructed by driving foundation stakes into the turf beneath the water and placing a platform on top. It is connected to the shore by an underground causeway which appears as a ridge of rock. The Picts are known to have been as small as pygmies and certainly only a race their size could survive on this tiny crannog which tradition associates with the 'little folk'.

During peaceful times the small population lived in communal 'wheel houses', segmented into rooms and earthed over. Many of these have now deteriorated into grassy mounds. They probably kept animals in nearby walled enclosures and grew crops in the surrounding land. In 84 AD the Romans attempted to invade Scotland. The Pictish tribes organised a massive resistance, pitting 'ferocious courage and outdated weapons against metal armour and disciplined experience'. Gradually the Roman opposition was eroded until they retreated behind Hadrian's Wall, leaving Scotland to be held by the Picts until the 3rd century. Originally there were many different Pictish tribes and Eigg was probably under the control of one based on the mainland in Moidart, but, as they slowly amalgamated into two, the Northern and Southern Picts, this situation could have changed.

In the middle of the 3rd century more people of Celtic origin began to infiltrate Scotland from Ireland. These 'Scots', as they came to be called, first inhabited Agyll or, as it was known then, Dalriada. Gradually they fought their way up the west coast defeating the Picts who, from the end of the 7th century, were also subject to raids from the Norse. Harried on every quarter, the Picts were driven underground and many of the legends connected with the 'little people' or 'fairies' are thought to derive from their guerrilla exploits against the enemy.

Eigg, in all likelihood, was used by both Pict and Scot as a convenient calling place. Before there were roads, island people lived in the mainstream of the known world. Their boats could carry them anywhere along the sea-paths, while the Western Isles were the last land before the sea stretched away in a great uncharted waste. Kenneth MacLeod says in *Songs of the Hebrides* that the interchange of ideas between those arriving and leaving and their accompanying 'spiritual drift-thought', laid the foundations for the Hebridean tradition of song and legend.

Pictish fortification on the Scurr with Lochan nam Ban Mora in the distance and the island of Rhum beyond

Celtic cross in Kildonnan graveyard

THE COMING
OF CHRISTIANITY

The Picts were pagan and their conversion to Christianity was the mission of the Irish monk, St Columba. A complex and erudite man, he left Ireland after a dispute in 693 and, together with twelve disciples, founded the monastery on Iona. This became the main spiritual centre and seat of learning in the Western Isles during a period when Celtic culture blossomed on both sides of the Irish Sea. These Celtic missionaries were remarkable not only for their learning but also for their evangelical zeal. They braved a foreign language and customs, wild weather, hunger and long, arduous journeys to take the Christian word to heathen Scotland.

St Columba was not the first to attempt a conversion of the Picts. St Ninian had already founded a monastery in 397 AD at Whithorn in Galloway called Candida Casa which became a training centre for missionary monks. St Donnan, who introduced the Christian religion to Eigg, trained at Whithorn. He was probably a Pict and certainly a follower of St Columba who warned him against any attempt to convert the people of Eigg because of the ferocity of their Pictish ruler. St Columba had travelled the Western seas and knew what St Donnan was likely to encounter. In Adamnan's life of St Columba it mentions that his mission extended to the islands of Islay, Mull, Coll, Tiree, Eigg and Skye, and indicates that he also visited the mainland. Allusions to 'Himba' are thought to refer to Canna, and Eigg is mentioned in one passage. It describes how, one day, St Columba had a spiritual revelation and regretted that his foster son Baithin – a cousin and his successor as Abbot of Iona – was not there to write it down because he was 'detained by winds in the Egean Island'.

It is always assumed on Eigg that St Columba did visit the island and drank from and blessed a well named after him in Cleadale. Kenneth Mac-Leod in *The Songs of the Hebrides* tells that St Columba's Well, *Tobar Challum Chille*, 'is fed by a burn running through the peat-moss and gets smaller and smaller in the days of drought, but never quite dries up. There are always tiny rivulets trickling over the rock into the Linn – just enough to baptise the children and keep the Faith alive, until the showers fall. In the number of these tricklets there are meanings. Are there nine? The child baptised under them becomes strong and beautiful as the nine rays of the sun, or as the ninth wave, the wave of healing, on the Laig strand after full tide. Are there seven? The child becomes a rover and adventurer, seeing through the weather of the seven elements the wonders of the seven days and the many seven years. Are there three tricklets? The child becomes like unto the Iona ones through the mystic symbol of the Triune, and has the knowledge of three Kingdoms, earth and sea and sky. But even in Eigg the numbers are not always sacred, and then the child grows up to be a common man, neither better nor worse than his neighbours, doing his day's work in the field or on the sea, with a place finally in St Donnan's churchyard'.

It is not known whether Baithin visited Eigg before or after St Donnan's mission. If it was before then his report may have contributed to St Columba's unease about the wisdom of St Donnan's proposal because when he called at Iona, on his way to Eigg, to make his confession and ask St Columba to be 'his soul's friend', he was told 'the corn must be ripe before the sickle may be laid to its root'. St Columba continued with the words,

'I will not confess thee, Donnan, for I am seeing the red blood of martyrdom about thine eyes'. In spite of this warning St Donnan set sail, for it is said, 'the constraint of three was upon Donnan, the constraint of the Evangel, the constraint of fate, and the constraint of his own blood; and to the Isle of Eigg he must needs to go, to preach the faith to the herdsmen of the Queen of Moydart, to whom pertained this isle as dainty pasture for her brindled cattle'.

Some accounts say that this queen used the island for grazing sheep. In *Celtic Scotland*, Skene records that 'The island of Eigg was probably at this time connected with this district as a pasture island reserved for their flocks of sheep', but goes on to say that 'while the people would seem to have been favourable to the little Christian colony established in the island by Donnan, the rule had passed into the hands of a woman who was still pagan'. This fearsome woman and her attendants, of reputed Amazonian proportions, also gave Eigg its alternative name of Island of Big Women. This name is always used at sea for, it was believed, if an island is called by its real name abroad the bad fairies hear and thereby discover its where-abouts. The English name of the lochan immediately below the Scurr, *Lochan nam Ban Mora*, is Loch of the Big Women. Some of the tribe are said to have inhabited this area and their ghosts haunt the place. One was seen recently, in September 1986. A group of five young people staying at the lodge were messing around on the crannog in the middle of the loch when they heard a wailing cry and looking up saw an enormous woman standing under the Scurr rock. She had long black hair, wore grey flowing garments and was waving her arms. At first the boys thought the figure was Keith Schellenberg up to one of his eccentric practical jokes. However, almost as soon as they registered the apparition, she vanished, and later, returning to the Lodge, they discovered Keith had a bad back and had not been out of the house all day.

The people of Eigg were practising pagans. A stone slab called *Leac an t-Sliasgaich* near Bealach Thuilm at the north end is believed to be just one of several sites of ancient pagan worship. Despite this they welcomed St Donnan when he arrived with fifty-two monks and set up his

A modern concrete statue of St Donnan

14

monastery at Kildonnan. To begin with they probably occupied the old Iron Age fort on the promontory but later they built a wooden church on the hill above on the site of the present grave-yard. The islanders gladly listened to St Donnan's Christian preaching and were further impressed when he exorcised the spirit of the dragon from the Massacre Cave. To perform this task St Donnan took holy water, two monks and the bravest of his island converts. He approached the cave, blessed the entrance and then ventured into the interior. Here he found none of the reputed stench the islanders claimed the dragons emitted but merely a skeleton which was thrown into the sea. After this the cave was prepared for use as a refuge.

The Queen of Moidart was furious when she heard the news of St Donnan's arrival and his conversions. She 'shook her head' and announced, 'I am keeping herdsmen to herd my milking cattle on the face of Corravine, and not to be herded themselves by a monk'. She sent word to Eigg by coracle that the monks should be put to death. 'But that was one thing under the sun the herdsmen would not do, even for the Queen of Moidart'

for they stated 'that would not be a religious act'. Whereupon, 'in a red hot rage', she dispatched a company of her own warriors to perform the deed.

Her pirate band landed on the 17th April, 617, and found St Donnan and his monks at Mass singing psalms in the Oratory. St Donnan requested that they should have 'respite until the Mass is ended'. When it was over, St Donnan, knowing that the pirates were powerless to hurt them while they were in the Oratory, said to his monks 'Let us go to the Refectory where we were wont to live after the flesh, and there we can be slain, for we cannot die so long as we remain where we were in the habit of pleasing God, but where we have been accustomed to nourish the flesh, there we may be loosed from the flesh.' In the Oratory they were 'murderously assailed' by the pirates and 'were slain every one of them'. So St Columba's prophecy was fulfilled and St Donnan and his fifty-two monks entered into red martyrdom.

At midnight, that night, they say a strange light shone upon the graves and voices from above chanted a croon:

The warm eye of Christ on the tomb of Donnan
The stars so high on the tomb of Donnan,
The warm eye of Christ on the tomb of Donnan,
No ill, no ill to the tomb of Donnan.

Early gives the sun greeting to Donnan
Early sings the bird the greatness of Donnan,
Early grows the grass on the grave of Donnan,
The warm eye of Christ on the grave,
The stars of the heavens on the grave,
No harm, no harm to Donnan's dust.

Recess in the medieval church at Kildonnan

The bones of St Donnan and his monks are believed to have been buried near the church in an oval, white, sandstone urn covered by a thin slab of red sandstone. The grave lay about one hundred yards north of the chapel in an arable field and the farmer used to leave that area unploughed. Martin Martin, in *Description of the Western Isles of Scotland, 1705*, says it was almost full of human bones and they were 'fair and dry', but there were no heads among them. He suggested that these were cut off 'with a two-handed sword and carried away by the enemy'. Doubt as to whether this was the actual grave site is cast by the Statistical Account of 1798 which mentions that the stone was exposed several years previously when the ground was being ploughed and 'upon which the urn, being a large, round, hollow stone, was taken up and examined and found to contain a number of bones, but no skull appeared among them. It was again buried, at the distance of a few yards from the place where it formerly lay', probably to remove it from harm. Until about fifty years ago the covering slab was open to view and could easily be raised. A superstition arose that if the gravestone was uncovered it rained without ceasing and, at times of protracted rain, the people used to go and see if the stone was exposed. If it was they would cover it over hoping that this would clear the skies. There is a story that at one time some men from Sleat who had come to have their corn ground at the mill on Eigg bared the Saint's gravestone to get water. They failed to cover the stone and 'it rained and rained and when they got back to Sleat they found their meal was spoiled'.

St Donnan's sacrifice was never forgotten on Eigg. The site of his monastery retains the name of Kildonnan or Church of Donnan. The 17th of April was kept as a holiday on the island until the 19th century and this poem commemorates his massacre.

With the festival of Peter the Deacon
To the glorious martyrdom ascended,
With his clerics, of pure lives,
Donnan of cold Eig.

The demise of St Donnan did not deter other saints from following him to Eigg and his monastery was soon re-occupied. The Annals of Ulster record the death of Oan, Superior of Eigg, in 724, and mentions another Abbot in 752 and also the names and days of other saints but not their dates. The monks who evangelised in the islands throve on solitude and loved nature. On the north shore of Eigg, at Tolain, some small, circular, beehive-shaped huts are thought to have been inhabited by hermits. They lived near the sea because their food came from the beach and they existed mainly on a diet of molluscs and seaweed. The aesthetic side of these monks is shown by their intricately carved sculptures and crosses. Several crosses may have been erected on Eigg although none survive. The main religious site was at Kildonnan but other places on the island were also used for preaching. Crosses probably marked these sites. In Cleadale, a place called *Druim-a-Chroisen* means site of a cross and another on the road to the shore, *Leaba' Chrabhaidh'* means place of devotion, and there were also crosses at Grulin and near Kildonnan Church. On Eigg they said that St Columba's disciples sang the following traditional hymn as they sailed amongst the islands:

The Catholic Church as it is today at Laig Bay

THE IONA RAINBOW

Oh Lord of the Heights, whose eye encircles
The land and the sea and smiles thro' the thunder.
Smile on us too, as we sail outward,
To far blue isles with tales and wonder
Of our Christ, our Crown, our song, our psalter.

Beyond those waves, strong hearts are longing
For Heaven's own tales, sweet wounds of the psalter.
Fair be our breeze, as outward we bear
Our Christ, our Crown, our song and our Altar
To far blue isles, sweet sounds of the psalter
Bear Christ, our Crown, our song, our Altar.

Iona shall grow 'mid far off oak trees,
The oak trees shall bear of love thou a-wakest,
Aloft in the sky Thy rainbow we see;
The Druid Thou mad'st, the Saint Thou remakst.
Bear Christ, our Crown, our song, our psalter.

Beside those waves, we kneel and praise Thee,
For wind and tide, for share of life's danger.
Well if at eve Iona we make,
E'en well tho' sleep we the sleep of the stranger.
Bear Christ, our Crown, our song, our Altar
To far blue isles sweet sounds of the psalter
Our Christ, our cross, our song, our Altar.

Early monasteries were self-governing units, each with their own rules and order of Mass. Their churches were small, designed to shelter the altar and priest, but not the congregation who worshipped in the open air. This lack of central organisation in Britain dismayed the Church of Rome who sought to regularise affairs and succeeded in doing so in 664 at the Synod of Whitby. The monks of Iona disagreed with the decision and continued to make their own rules until 722 when pressure forced them to capitulate. However, the old habits died slowly in remote areas of the north and it was not until the 12th century that Roman rule was generally accepted. By that time the niceties of Roman law were of little matter compared to the attacks they were receiving from another quarter. The Vikings, pagan in religion and philistine in deed, began raiding the Western Isles from the end of the 7th century onwards. They sacked every monastery in their path, including the church on Eigg which was twice burnt to the ground. Their desecrations destroyed the work of the Celtic missionaries who were 'the first to offer the satisfaction of a real religion to a pagan people who were sensitive to spiritual forces' and ended effective religion on Eigg until the 16th century.

The reason for the success of the early Christian missionaries was that they did not try to wean the people from their pagan beliefs but rather grafted Christianity onto its stock. This strange mixture of religion and superstition underlies island beliefs to this day. Its endurance was aided by the fact that for three centuries after the Vikings departed in the 13th century the people were left without teachers, books or any real written language. During this time, Christian and pagan roots became inextricably entwined. Gods and spirits were transformed into demons or given witches' powers once possessed by the Druids. The creation of myths was helped by the lack of communication with the outside world; nights in winter were long and filled with stories passed from one generation to the next, where the fancy of the teller became mixed with the fact of the tale. Their lives were dominated by the rhythm of their work, the movement of the herds out to pasture in spring, their return to the stubbles in autumn, the sowing and reaping of crops, the migration of the herring shoals, and the recurrent sequence of events within the family: births, marriages and deaths. Nothing much changed except the weather and its behaviour affected their whole existence.

The appearance of the sun after days of dark and dampness must have seemed a blessed thing and worth worshipping. On Eigg the islanders' belief in its power can be seen to this day. Coffins are paraded 'deasil', or sunwise, once round the old church at Kildonnan before being laid in the grave. They say it is done for luck but the habit has its origins in pagan worship of Grannos or Gruagach, the 'fair-haired' sun god. An ancient reverence for the moon was displayed by the way its phases dominated certain activities. Peats were cut when it was on the wane because if the chore was performed when the moon was waxing they would 'give neither light nor heat but only the power of smoke'.

Certain Christian precepts were given a local slant. Hell was assumed to be cold rather than hot. A realistic idea, says Hugh MacDiarmid in his book *The Islands of Scotland*. 'In a land of damp and draughts, and wet mist and low-lying clouds, a warm hell sounds almost luxurious'. The people have a saying which one soon learns to appreciate, 'Hell is bitter with its dampness'. The sinful were taken there on a fire ship which was sometimes seen by the gifted ones on Eigg. It careered past the Isle at frightening speed, 'and on deck was a long, lean, black creature with a fiddle in his hand, ever playing and dancing and laughing' while 'awful was the howling that was below'. Heaven, named Tir-nan-Og or Land of the Ever Young, was also thought to be situated somewhere in the western seas where the sun sets.

It used to be said that 'The Celtic soul ever waits on the shore of the great Sea for the coming of the White Barge which, year in year out, ferries the elect across the waves to the Isle where they would be. And that same Barge needs neither wind nor sail nor rudder to make her speed like a bird over the sea; the wish of the Fate that guides her all and her in all.' The ship, riding the waves like a queen, could be seen by the pure in heart on days when 'the dawn was clear as dew, the sky green as the green of moonrise, and the sea blue as the blue of wonder', and to this heaven they composed a song:

TIR-NAN-OG

The roar of the waves, plaintive their sound,
As they chant in my ear thy praise,
The song of the bens, the fountain and stream,
With thy music downward flow;
By day my witchment ever thou art,
Thy longing eternal me wounds,
And by night thou art ever my dream,
O Tir-nan-Og.

Death nor sorrow in thy Beauty-land lives,
In the grave are deceit and guile,
The brave ever drink of thy generous life,
Gladness swims in the clouds;
Lofty stars by day and by night
Shine softly through a mist,
Mellowist harps grow up in thy woods,
O Tir-nan-Og.

Behind the waves, the ship of my dream
Goes sailing as of yore,
The wish of Fate ever speeds her way
Silent and swift as a bird;
White Barge, O leave me not in distress
On the shore of mighty seas,
Depths in pain and love me song-draw
To Tir-nan-Og.

Each day of the week had special significance. Thursday on Eigg was especially good for working with sheep and cattle. The reason for this custom is recorded by Alexander Carmichael in *Carmina Gadelica.* One day St Columba was passing by the 'Island of Women' in his coracle when an old woman ran down to the water's edge and cried to him, 'Columba, Columba, thou art the world's head of wisdom and healing'. St Columba asked what ailed her and she told him that her husband had died 'on the strand of periwinkles' and her son was drowned swimming to the Isle of Women to see his mother and she was left with three orphan children and a lovely little heifer who would not give milk for the children nor take her own calf and 'I know not under the white sun what to do'. St Columba said, 'I have made prattlings of cows and incantations of horses in my day and generation. I had them in a skin book and the skin book was in the window and the skin book was stolen from me, so I have no charms available this day. But I will make a rune for you, poor woman, and thou shalt sing it to thy heifer. So Columba made her a rune and she sang it to the heifer and the heifer took to her calf and gave milk, and so the Day of St Columba is the day of blessings on flocks and herds, for great was St Columba with all beasts.

Throughout the year certain festivals were celebrated and special bannocks were baked on that day. The Festival of St Bride, on the 1st February, was said to date back to the worship of Brid, the Fire Goddess, but became transmuted into a reverence for St Bride. She was believed to be the aid-woman of Mary at the birth of Christ, to preside over art and all beauty beneath the sky and sea, and to oversee the seasons, giving them their functions. The venom of cold trembled for

its safety on St Bride's Day and the sea became warmer because she dipped her hand in its depths. At Beltane, on the 1st May, the cattle were moved out to the spring pasture. St Michael's Day, on the 29th September, was observed with ritual. Hallowe'en, on the 31st October, marked the end of the half year of long days and the beginning of the dark, cold, second half. On that night witches and other dubious beings were especially powerful. At Samhain, 1st November, the cattle returned for the winter and peat fires, covered or smoored every evening and kept alight throughout the year, were extinguished. The new one was lit from a communal bonfire and this 'need fire' dates back to an ancient rite designed to prevent cattle plague when the cattle were driven round the bonfire to keep them from harm during the year. More ancient ritual survives in Hogmanay or New Year's Eve, celebrated by the time-honoured habit of first-footing and drams of whisky. The idea behind this is to bless the house and wish for plenty of food in the coming year.

After the Reformation of 1560 the Church discouraged many of the old beliefs and festivals, only approving of Christmas, Easter, Good Friday and St Michael's Day. However, the people on Eigg, because they retained the Catholic faith and with it a relative independence from the more rigid strictures of the Protestant church, maintained the traditional customs and their myths. Indeed, a strong element of fear and superstition survives even to this day.

THE REIGN
OF THE VIKINGS

Eigg, along with all the other Hebridean islands, was subject to piratical raids by the Vikings from the end of the 7th century. Then, in 880 Harald Harfanger proclaimed himself King of Norway and his most virulent opponents, seeking to escape his rule, left Norway and began settling the Scottish isles, using them as bases from which to attack Norway. King Harald pursued these renegades, succeeded in subduing them in 888 and added the Hebrides to the crown of Norway. The Vikings continued to revolt, but in 890 they were reduced to obedience by an emissary of Harald's, Kentil Flatneb. He then turned coat, ingratiated himself with the chief islanders and declared himself King of the Isles and independent of Norway. This title was disputed by Norway and, over the next two centuries, they fought for control of the Hebrides.

The Norse conquest did not materially affect the character, language or social institutions of the majority of the Celtic population. The 19th-century historian, Gregory, states 'that in all cases of conquest the changes in the population must have been most perceptible in the higher ranks, owing to the natural tendency of the invaders to secure their new positions when practicable by matrimonial alliance with the natives'. The Norse did introduce a new system of land tenure and rents were paid according to whether you possessed farthing land, penny land or merk land. Their influence can also be seen in the huge number of Norse place names to be found all over the Hebrides.

Eigg was no exception to this rule. Everywhere, place names have Norse origins. Laig, for instance, means 'roaring of the surf', the name coming from the sound of the waves beating the broad strand below the farm. The Norse also left many relics, particularly at Laig and Kildonnan, showing that they took up residence in these already established settlements.

Viking remains were found in the field below Kildonnan Church when it was levelled down in 1830 and, in 1875, a determined dig was made of two Viking burial mounds. The first grave contained an ornate sword hilt, iron axe head, sickle, cast-iron cauldron leg, pieces of linen and woollen material, amber beads, spindle whorl, iron belt clasp and a bronze penannular thistle brooch used by Viking women in the 10th century to secure their dresses. The second, smaller grave, revealed a bronze brooch, jet beads and part of an iron sword. Another grave, marked by a 'huge limb of rough stone', situated below the road south of the Scurr, had arrow heads and amber beads, and all of these objects are now on display in the National Museum of Antiquities in Edinburgh.

It is thought that the marshy area below Laig farm was once an inland lake joined to the sea by a canal and used by the Norse as a winter harbour and boat-building yard. When the area was drained around 1870, oaken logs were found lying thirty feet apart which were the prow and stern posts of an uncompleted Viking boat. The remains of the canal can still be seen and 600 yards from this there is a place called *Sron Laimhrige* which translated means headland or landing place.

During the 9th century the Norse kings turned their attention towards the richer haul of England

and neglected their Scottish possessions. It was not until King Magnus Barefoot was defeated by King Harold at Stamford Bridge in 1066 that their interest was revived. Godred Coven, who led the Norwegian army into battle and was married to the Norse king's daughter, fled to the west. Here he proceeded to form an army with which he expelled the King of the Isles of Mann, subjugated a large part of Ireland, and then marched on mainland Scotland and its king, Malcolm III. The Islesmen seem to have readily accepted Coven and his ambitions, perhaps because he was a great character, and celebrated his eventful life in song and legend.

However, Magnus Barefoot was not impressed by Coven's exploits and in 1093 invaded the Isles, unseated Coven and, in his place, substituted his son Sigurd. When Magnus died in 1103 Sigurd returned to Norway and the islanders took Lagman, Coven's eldest son, for their king. He abdicated in order to make a pilgrimage to Jerusalem where he died. His brother Olaf then assumed the crown until he was defeated by the Irish Gael, Somerled.

Little is known of Somerled's beginnings, beyond the fact that he was born in the first decade of the 12th century, was of Irish extraction and must early have proved himself a leader as the Dalriadans chose him to help them in their struggles against the Norse. In those days a chief did not always succeed by hereditary right but had to be accepted by the clan, proving by his character, purpose and skill at arms that he had the necessary strength to keep their kingdom together during this age of constant war. Somerled, it is told, was more interested in hunting and fishing than kingship and was reluctant to accept the leadership. He reached his decision after spending several days fishing for a particularly fine salmon. On the final day he made a deal with his clansmen that, if he caught the fish, he would take their challenge and lead them in battle. He hooked the salmon, kept his promise, altered Scottish history and, to this day, the salmon forms part of the quarterings on the Clan Donald arms.

Somerled, described by the Sleat historian as being 'A well-tempered man, in body shapely, of a fair piercing eye, of middle stature and of quick discernment' and by others as 'the greatest hero that his race has produced', was immediately successful against the Norse. In his first action, seeing that his forces were smaller than those of the enemy, he decided to try and deceive the Norse by a cunning ruse. He paraded his men several times in their sight, each time taking them out of sight behind a hill, changing their clothes and allowing them to re-emerge from a different point. Then he led a spirited charge; the Norse were driven into confusion and retreated to their ships with many men and two of their chiefs dead.

As he won more battles, Somerled's influence rose; he assumed the title Lord of Argyll and became one of the most powerful chiefs in Scotland. He then turned his attention to the Isles, seeking to ally himself with their hierarchy by a dynastic marriage, requesting the hand of Ragnhilda, the daughter of King Olaf the Red. Olaf refused, haughtily telling Somerled that she was destined for a man of far higher rank. Somerled bided his time, waiting for a chance to prove his superiority. It came when Olaf, on a voyage north, lay at anchor in the lea of Ardnamurchan Point. Somerled also happened to be anchored in the same bay and a skilful shipwright in his crew, Maurice MacNeil, conceived a devious plan to make Olaf see reason. MacNeil swam across to Olaf's galley under cover of darkness, bored several holes along the starboard stake and stuffed them with tallow. The next morning both chiefs set sail for Skye, but as they rounded the headland, in the pitch and roll of the Atlantic swell, the tallow gave way and Olaf's galley began to sink. Olaf hailed Somerled and asked for help but Somerled refused until he agreed to his marriage to Ragnhilda. Once the promise was given MacNeil dived down and plugged the holes with wooden pins. In 1140 Somerled married Ragnhilda and from this union all MacDonalds can claim descent.

Marriage did not abate Somerled's taste for battle and new land and he continued to attack the mainland of Scotland and the Isle of Man, ruled by King Godred. In January 1156 Somerled fought a bloody battle against Godred off the north coast of Islay. It continued all night, and when day dawned and both sides were exhausted, a treaty was reached whereby Somerled took all the isles south of Ardnamurchan and Godred retained those north of the peninsula which would have included Eigg. Somerled did not respect the treaty for long and, two years later, he invaded Man with fifty-three ships, defeating Godred who fled to Norway.

By 1158 Somerled effectively controlled the Western Isles and Dalriada, although officially he held the islands from the King of Norway and his mainland territory from the King of Scotland. Unofficially, Somerled acted as an independent prince and treated both kings as inconvenient sovereigns of distant lands. This attitude prevailed amongst the Lords of the Isles for many centuries.

Somerled was murdered in his tent in 1164 while raiding the Clyde in an attempt to conquer the whole of Scotland. His troops, deprived of their leader, were routed in battle and hastily retired to the Western Isles and his kingdom was divided between his legitimate children. The eldest, Dugall, inherited Lorn, Mull and Jura; Reginald received the main seats of power, Islay and Kintyre; and the youngest, Angus, got Bute, part of Arran and Garmoran or Rough Bounds. The latter comprised all the territory stretching from Ardnamurchan to Glenelg, and included Eigg. Reginald coveted the Garmoran properties and attacked Angus in 1192. He lost the battle but, in 1210, fought Angus again, probably in Moidart, and this time Reginald won and Angus and his three sons were killed 'by the men of Skye'.

Reginald was now the most powerful man in the Western Isles and his seal grandly describes him as Reginaldus Rex Insularium Dominus de Argile. He married the daughter of the influential Earl of Moray and had three sons, all of whom founded dynastic clans. Dougall, who founded the Clan MacDougal; Donald, whose progeny became the MacDonalds, hereditary Lords of the Isles, and Ruarie from whom the MacRuaries are descended. Ruarie, who acquired Bute, part of Kintyre and the Small Isles, was a wild and restless man with all the wandering, seafaring temperament of his forebears. With Argyll, Ruarie had a power and position rivalled only by Donald and together they formed an unbeatable team, strong enough to barrack repeated attempts by the Scots crown to bring their western properties under some form of control. Throughout the 13th century royal forces brutally raided the islands. In 1262 they 'sacked villages and desecrated churches' and 'in wanton fury raised children on the points of their spears and shook them until they fell to the ground'.

The power of Norway was beginning to crumble. But when the Scottish crown invaded the Kingdom of Man, and Haakon of Norway called for help, Donald and Ruarie, who still considered themselves nominal vassals of that country, obliged. They defeated the Scottish army 'with great slaughter', but during their absence their Scottish neighbours took the opportunity of invading Bute and threatening their other properties. Ruarie sailed to Norway to seek assistance. Haakon marshalled a force and, early in 1263, sailed with an armada of ships. They joined forces with other island chiefs at Kererra and routed the intruders. Victorious, they were not slow to seek revenge on their enemies and 'plundered and wasted with fire and sword' many miles of country. This imprudence at a late time of year was their undoing. September storms, supposedly raised by witches, and an unexpected resistance at Largs during an attack on Ayrshire, forced them to retire to the Orkneys. Here Haakon died, and taking advantage of their leaderless position Alexander III resumed his attacks. In 1265 Haakon's son Magnus capitulated; the Western Isles were ceded to Scotland provided an annual sum was paid to Norway, that all Norwegian subjects who wished could freely

leave the country, and that no islanders were punished for their collaboration.

The Norse left but their ghosts remained. On Eigg the field below Kildonnan containing Viking burial mounds became known as the Field of Fairy Knolls, *Dail Sithean*, and was believed to be haunted by people who came down from the Scurr lochs. In 1875, when archaeologists made excavations, the islanders were reluctant to help. A very tall man, dressed all in green and thought to be a Viking, has been seen standing on top of the largest of several mounds lying below Galmisdale House. The last sighting was by an army Major who rented the house from the Runcimans during this century. Sir Steven says there is reason to believe the story as the Major was not the type of man given to fancy. 'He was a typical Major with handlebar moustache and no more imagination than a table'. One day he was standing outside the front door looking through his binoculars when he saw a very tall man dressed in a green plaid, stockings and hat. He called to his wife to come and look out, but as she did so, the man vanished. The Major reported the incident to the gamekeeper but was too ashamed to tell the Runcimans, thinking that people like him did not see ghosts. The gamekeeper told Sir Steven Runciman and when asked if anyone else had ever seen the green man said he would inquire. Eventually, his bed-ridden mother admitted that her father had seen him about a hundred years before.

Yet another man is seen crossing the bridge over the burn at the bottom of the lodge drive, often with a dog at his heels. He is also thought to be a Viking because on the other side of the burn there is a desecrated grave. Anybody crossing the bridge late in the evening gets an odd feeling and hurries by. This Viking was definitely seen by the district nurse, a very practical woman who was taking a short cut through the lodge grounds at night after visiting a sick cottager by the pier during the Runciman's day. Suddenly she was aware of a tall man crossing the bridge. 'She felt funny all over and hurried on.'

Fairies haunt mounds at Laig where two of them beside the farmhouse are traditionally known as The Great Sithean, *An Sithean Mor*, and the Hag's Sithean, *Sithean na Cailleich*. Another ugly fairy gives its name to a mound at the end of Cnoc Oilteig Farm, which translated means 'hill of the ugly one'. It is said to be always ready to assist the occupants on nightly excursions to visit neighbours. There are mounds on Castle Island which are said to be named after a 'giant' who lived here and built a castle.

Kenneth MacLeod, in *Songs of the Hebrides*, describes how the 'mound dwellers' were thought to have a 'soft, sorrowful' music of their own which was borrowed by the Gaelic-speaking dwellers above ground whenever they got a chance. In many folk tales there are descriptions of 'slender women of the green kirtles and yellow hair' singing lullabies and love songs. The fairy folk were said to be so good at music that 'the sapling might become the tallest tree in the forest before you would get tired of listening', and the lads on the island would go down to the knolls on moonlit nights to hear the piping. Bending an ear to the knoll 'It was tunes they would get, and tunes indeed; reels that would make the Merrydancers themselves go faster, and laments that would draw tears from the eyes of a corpse; sure in one night, a lad o' music might get as many reels and laments as would marry and bury all the people in Eigg – ay, and in the whole Clanranald country forbye'.

THE LORDS
OF THE ISLES

After King Haakon's death, the Hebrides, although nominally restored to the Scottish crown, continued to maintain a lawless independence. Their remote position on the western seaboard and the wildness of the country that separated them from the seat of Government made them almost impossible to control. This situation was aided by the fact that the political loyalties of the Scots establishment were divided. The MacDonalds of the Isles allotted their allegiance as seemed most expedient. Donald's son, Angus Mor, allied himself with Robert the Bruce in his dispute with John Balliol, vassal of Edward I of England, over who should wear the Scottish crown. Ruarie's son, Alan, was rewarded for his loyalty to King Alexander with the gift of Barra, Uist, Harris and the lesser islands of Eigg and Rhum. Alan was present when the Scottish Estates assembled at Scone in 1284 and declared Margaret, Maid of Norway, heiress to the throne. He died shortly after and, passing over the claims of several sons, left all his land to his daughter Christina. She was related by marriage to Robert Bruce and helped him on several occasions, lending him men, silver and food, and giving him refuge on her lands when he was forced to flee the mainland.

Christina's half-brother, Ruarie, fought for Robert Bruce at Bannockburn and contributed to his victory. The English were already in disarray when Bruce brought up his reserves. He instructed a company of Islesmen to assist Edward Bruce on the right of the battle with the words 'My hope is constant in thee'. These words were later incorporated into the arms of the Clanranald chiefs. Ruarie was rewarded for his services with land in Argyll, 'a davoch and a half of Moidart, half a davoch of Arisaig, the six davoch lands of Eigg and Rum, with the patronage of the Church of Kildonnan in Eigg, the six davochs and three-quarter of the land in Kilpeter in South Uist, the whole of Barra and Harris', resigned to him by Christina. He was killed at the battle of Dundalk in Ireland in 1318 and succeeded by his son Ranald who, in spite of changing political sides several times during his life according to the prevailing climate, was eventually murdered by Scots Barons and died without issue. His lands were given to his brother Alan and when he died soon after, to his sister Amie. She married John, Lord of the Isles, in 1337, and added her land to his considerable properties. John was an ambitious man and no less political than his forebears. He was taken prisoner by the English at the Battle of Poitiers, managed to escape to Scotland, backed David II's claims to the Scottish throne and then, anxious to consolidate his position, abandoned Amie to marry Margaret, daughter of the future Robert II. He was made Steward of Scotland and, when Robert ascended to the throne, one of his first actions was to confirm his 'beloved son, John of Isla, in the 300 merklands, once the property of Alan, the son of Ruarie, namely the lands of Moidart, Arisaig, Morar, Knoydart, being in the lordship of Garmoran; also the Islands of Uist, Barra, Rhum and Eigg, and Harris, being part of Lewis', on 9th March 1372. Neither Amie, who was described as 'a good and virtuous gentlewoman' and took to the religious life after her divorce, nor her two sons, Ranald and Godfrey, received any notice of this arbitrary redistribution of their land. However, on John's death in 1386, the situation was somewhat rectified and although Donald, the eldest of his three sons by Margaret, inherited the title of

Lord of the Isles and most of the land, that brought to him by his marriage to Amie was bequeathed to their sons. Ranald, in spite of the fact that he was the legitimate heir, had little option but to accept the terms as Donald's claim was supported by the King and confirmed by Royal Charter in 1373.

The ceremonial handing over by Ranald, as High Steward of the Isles, of all the rights and privileges of the Lordship of the Isles to Donald, took place on Eigg in 1386 in the presence of 'all the nobles of the Islands and his brethren'. Ranald 'gave the sceptre to his brother at Cill Donnan on Eigg who was nominated MacDonald and Donald of Isla, contrary to the opinion of the men of the Islands . . . Donald took the Lordship with the consent of his brethren and the nobles of the Islands, all other persons being obedient to him'. This processional hymn is then said to have been sung.

Nal-la vo hi! Like the rising sun,
Nal-la vo ha! Putting darkness on the stars.
Nal-la vo hi! My King's son in his armour,
Ro-va ha! With his spotted, speckled shield.
Nal-la vo hi! White his spear-head gleaming,
Nal-la vo ha! Swift his arrows in their flight.
Nal-la vo hi! Great galleys sailing
Nal-la vo ha! Hero he like to Cuchulan,
O hi, Like the rising sun!
Nal-la vo ha! Nal-la vo hi!

Captain Ranald Macdonald, the present chief of Clanranald

The nomination of Lord of the Isles normally took place at Finlaggan on Eilean Mor and Eigg was probably chosen on this occasion, partly because the island belonged to the MacRuarie family, and by attending the ceremony and publicly handing over his rights on Eigg, Ranald showed his acquiesence to Donald, and partly because the island's central position made it a convenient meeting place. The ceremony of the installation of the Lords of the Isles followed a formal pattern. On Finlaggan there is a well-marked stone with a foot-mark cut in it where the chief stood when, before the 'gentlemen of the Islands' he was proclaimed 'MacDonald' and 'High-prince of the seed of Conn'. No such stone has been found on Eigg and it may be that he stood on a cairn of stones surrounded by his followers. The ceremony was completed by a Mass and then a week of feasting. The government of the Lords of the Isles had an exact constitution. A council of sixteen met regularly round a stone table at Finlaggan while every island had a judge for 'the discussion of all controversies' of those who held land from MacDonald.

From this time on, Ranald held Rhum, Morar, Arisaig, Eigg and half of South Uist, while Godfrey had the other half of South Uist, North Uist, Benbecula, Boisdale, Canna, Sleat and Knoydart. His lands were seized by Ranald on Godfrey's death, because his sons were minors, and thus the Chieftainship of the MacDonalds of Clanranald was established.

The Chieftainship of a Highland clan was based on Celtic laws and customs; the chief was head of the whole name while a chieftain was head of an established branch. Clans were composed of closely interrelated family groups owing loyalty to their chieftain who was considered to be their father and whose authority was unassailable. He dealt with criminal and civil cases and, as a matter of honour, avenged all injuries to the life and property of the family. Although the clans held together as social unities the chieftains maintained interminable vendettas against each other, calling out their men for prolonged and bloody wars. They organised cattle raiding and wife stealing, murder and betrayal so that for centuries cruelty and tragedy were inescapable parts of the lives of their clansmen.

Chieftains were pledged to give assistance to their chiefs in times of war. The Clanranalds were obliged to provide a twenty-six-oared galley, complete with men and provisions, to the Lords of the Isles. The war galley was derived from the Norsemen's boats, with high stem and stern, light draught, banks of oars and square sail which enabled it to skim over the water. The islanders' ships were so formidable that as he lay dying Robert the Bruce warned his son of them and official English reports bear witness to their extreme fitness for fighting in the narrow west-coast seas. Until the end of the 16th century each chieftain kept a galley and crew 'ready for any enterprise or piratical expedition in which the west coast Highlanders excelled'. The 18th-century Eigg Bard, Alexander Macdonald, composed a famous sea-poem describing Clanranald's Galley.

THE BIRLINN OF CLANRANALD

English after Sheriff Nicholson's translation

Father of ocean,
Bless our birlinn,
Sweep smooth the waves,
Our port draw nigh.
Bless all our mast-hoops
Our ropes and halyards,
May no evil e'er to them come nigh
And you our crew brave deeds encounter!
Speed our birlinn black and shapely,
Bulging sea-glens
Piled before us
Blinded by the spray of surges,
Watching well the briny storm-hills
Hoist we sail from Uist of wild geese,
Oars a twisting billows curling
Thrust our galley hissing through sea-glens
Fire-balls blazing high i' the rigging
Full the deep of crawling spectres,
Seals all torn and great sea-monsters,
All a-howling, screeching, groaning,
Drag us all a-board your birlinn,
Drive the mountain monsters onward,
Pounding grey backed swirling eddies,
Send the surge in sparkles skyward,
Hoary-headed seas up-swelling.

Donald was a good man and proved himself a worthy holder of the title, Lord of the Isles. He ended his days in a Benedictine monastery and was followed by his son, Alexander, who was succeeded by his son John, a meek and modest man. John was brought up in the Scots court and became a scholar 'more fit to be a churchman than to command so many irregular tribes of people'. He endeavoured to keep their allegiance 'by bestowing gifts on some, and promoting others with lands and possessions; by this he became prodigal and very expensive', which unequal policy created dissension amongst the Islesmen. John's offspring consisted of two illegitimate sons and increasingly the islanders looked to one, Angus, for a lead and influence on his father. He did not have much effect and in 1493 the weak-willed John formally forfeited his title and estates to James IV and spent the rest of his life at court living on a pension and running up expenses which were paid for by the King, no doubt in return for his allegiance.

Civil war erupted between Angus and his followers and the island chiefs who accepted the King's rule. A battle was fought at Bloody Bay on the north-west coast of Mull, which Angus won, but the enmity continued and a feud existed between the MacLeods of Harris and Skye and the MacDonalds of Clanranald which was to have profound consequences for Eigg. Angus was murdered during a raid against the Argylls after they had kidnapped his three-year-old son, Donald Dubh. In an effort to silence any claim Donald Dubh might make to the Lordship, the Argylls kept him a prisoner in Inch Connell Castle on an island in Loch Awe 'until his hair got grey'. The islands were in a turmoil. After Angus died the Highlanders and Islanders ran 'loose, and began to shed one another's blood'. The Government were unable to effectively control the Western Isles until they had achieved naval supremacy. They could break the islands' independence but they could not produce a stable government. Their weakness was evident in every repressive action to which the islanders retaliated with 'rebellion' and 'treason'. In 1502 they nominated Donald Dubh Lord of the Isles and rescued him from imprisonment. Donald Dubh,

a man of intrepid courage, who had preserved an unbroken spirit in spite of prolonged injustice and adversity, led a series of uprisings against James V until he was recaptured and incarcerated in Edinburgh Castle.

In 1543 Donald Dubh escaped again and, in a last desperate effort to raise more funds and support, called a conference on Eigg. Here a Commission was drawn up to 'treat with the King of England', Henry VIII, and an announcement was issued that:

'We Donald Lord of ye Isles ... with advise and consent of air barronis and counseill of ye Ilis ... giffard our full power express bidding and command to ... all and haill ye saidis Commissionaris ... and in special testifying our Landis instantlie be maid to ane nobill and potent prince Harye ye Acht.'

The Commissioners met Henry VIII who donated 1,300 crowns to their cause but it was of little avail. Delays and quarrels about the distribution of the finance led to the collapse of the venture and, soon after, Donald Dubh died of fever at Drogheda in Ireland. His death ended the direct line of the Lords of the Isles.

The Scottish crown did not abandon its attempts to control the Western Islanders, encouraging disputes between the clans on the basis of 'divide and rule'. A state of anarchy resulted from 'the constant endeavours of kings to impose their authority on people who recognised only that of their chiefs and on chiefs who recognised none'. Feuds which would have been smoothed over by the Lords of the Isles were allowed to fester and the clan as a warring band dates from this time.

The most vicious attack on Eigg occurred in 1577. The event has come down in the annals of Eigg as one of the most momentous and tragic episodes in the island's history. Accounts vary, and none were written until at least a century later, but it is generally agreed that the episode began in March at a time when the MacDonalds were feuding with the MacLeods over some land they claimed on Skye. It all started when a party of MacLeods, returning to Skye, were forced into Eigg by bad weather. They landed on Castle Island, stupidly molested some girls tending the cattle and were seen by men on Eigg. They crossed to Castle Island, seized the MacLeods and after thrashing them, or some say chopping off their hands, tied them up, bound them to the benches of their boat and cast it adrift. Fortunately for the MacLeods the tide carried them in the direction of Skye and, nearing the coast, they were seen and rescued. When news of the occurrence reached their chief, Alistair Crotach of Dunvegan, he vowed vengeance and manning his galleys set sail for Eigg. Their approach was seen by some men on Eigg carrying a huge column of pitchstone porphry rock from the Scurr to the graveyard at Kildonnan. They dropped the stone, where it still lies by the roadside, a few hundred yards from the graveyard, and alerted the other islanders. Feeling that they did not have enough men to offer resistance, because many of their number were away on a boat crew in Glasgow, the remaining islanders retreated into the St Francis, *Uamh Fhraing*, cave on the south-west side of Eigg. This enormous cavern, formed by wave action on a fault in the basalt rock, has a tunnel-like entrance extending for some 12 feet before opening up into the main chamber measuring 213 feet long, 22 feet broad and 17 feet high.

Into this cave the 365 islanders retreated except for one old woman who hid herself in a cave at the north end of the island. The MacLeods landed on Port nam Partan beach, searched the island for two to three days, found it apparently deserted and, disappointed and enraged, burned houses and destroyed crops until they finally discovered the old woman. Alistair Crotach said he would not stain his hands with her blood but he would deprive her of all means of subsistence and ordered the sands of Kildonnan to be ploughed to destroy the razor fish which was all he thought remained for her to eat. Hearing what had been done, the old lady announced that 'as long as I can get dulse from the hollow at Talm, the soft watercress and a drink from the well at Howlin that will suffice'.

The MacLeods then prepared to leave when they caught sight of a man on the horizon. He was a scout who had been sent out to reconnoitre the situation. Unfortunately, a light snow had fallen which allowed the MacLeods to trace his footsteps back to the cave. Alistair Crotach shouted into the entrance that if those who had ill-treated his men were given up, the other islanders would be spared. 'Shrieks of despair' were heard from within but his request was refused, the Macdonalds preferring to perish together rather than betray one of their number. The MacLeods then decided to light a huge bonfire at the cave's entrance and smoke the inhabitants to death. They gathered up all the inflammable materials they could find, including the thatch and furniture from nearby cottages, piled it against the entrance and were about to set it alight when Alistair Crotach, a religious man, had doubts about the idea and told them to stop. He decided to pray for guidance, announcing that if, at the end of six hours, the wind was blowing off the

The St Francis Cave, now known as the Massacre Cave

mouth of the cave the people would be spared. When he had finished the wind was blowing full on its mouth. Alistair Crotach saw this as a sign from heaven but, even so, was unable to commit the deed, leaving it to his son William to light the fire. The smoke billowed into the cave and every 'man, woman and bairn' suffocated and died.

Judging from the narrow entrance of the cave, and the huge draughty cavern beyond, it seems more likely that the fire did not so much smoke the inhabitants to death as draw out the oxygen and they were extinguished as a candle flame under an upturned jar. Whatever happened, visitors to the cave in later centuries report finding 'many miserable relics of the victims'. The Revd. Donald MacLean wrote in 1788 that 'In the confined air of this cave, the bones are still pretty fresh, and some of the skulls entire, and the teeth in their sockets. About forty skulls have been lately numbered here. It is probable a greater number were destroyed; if so, their neighbouring friends may have carried them off for burial in consecrated ground'. In 1841 Mr James Wilson, in his *Voyage round the Coasts of Scotland*, mentions finding 'a few teeth . . . sticking fast in a

fragment of jaw' while Hugh Miller said, after a visit in 1846, that 'Never yet was tragedy enacted in a gloomier theatre', and that 'the floor . . . resembles that of a charnel house. At almost every step we come upon heaps of human bones grouped together . . . the skulls, with the exception of a few broken fragments, have disappeared; for travellers in the Hebrides have of late years been numerous and curious; and many a museum . . . exhibits, in a grinning skull, its memorial of the Massacre of Eigg'. Sir Walter Scott was one such souvenir hunter and a skull from Eigg was displayed at Abbotsford. Lawrence Thompson, proprietor of Eigg in the late 19th century, decided to bury what remained of the bones but gave them a protestant service which infuriated the islanders. Today visitors to the cave find nothing but a dank gloom, its clamminess exaggerated by the memory of the events of the massacre. The old lady who was spared is said to haunt the bridge over the burn at the bottom of Kildonnan Hill.

The island was quickly re-populated, probably by the Clanranald moving in people from his other properties, and the feud with the MacLeods continued. The Macdonalds proved they could give in as brutal fashion as they got when, some time later, a party of MacDonalds from Uist raided Skye in revenge for the Eigg massacre. They landed on the promontory of Ardmore, found the MacLeods of Vaternish in church and set it alight. As the MacDonalds stood around enjoying the spectacle with 'savage glee' they forgot that the rising smoke would act as a signal. Their galleys had also been seen from Dunvegan from where the firey cross was sent round and the Clan MacLeod converged on the scene. The MacDonalds rushed for their boats but the tide had retreated leaving them high up the beach. In desperation they pulled them down the strand but 'with every moment their assailants increased and soon a desperate encounter took place and every MacDonald was slain'. Their bodies were ranged in a long row beneath a turf dyke and the sods 'turned over on them'.

Some years later revenge was sought for this defeat. MacCulloch in *The Misty Isles of Skye* describes how the MacDonalds raided the MacLeod's cattle on Skye. At daybreak the thieves were overtaken near Trumpan and a bloody fight ensued during which Roderick, son of Ian MacLeod of Unish, executed his sword with great bravery. A MacDonald had rushed him and cut off his legs at the knees but the doughty clansman continued to stand on his stumps cutting down all-comers. The fight continued until only two

blacksmiths in full armour remained in the fray. The MacLeod blacksmith was failing through lack of blood when his wife arrived at the scene and cried 'Turn to me' but, as he turned his head, the MacDonald ran him through with his sword and he died.

Further atrocities were perpetrated when, in 1588, Sir Lachlan MacLean of Duart raided Eigg with the help of a hundred Spaniards; the crew of a galleon called the *Juan de Sicilia*, which escaped the English after the Armada, sailed up the Scottish coast and sank in Tobermory Harbour on Mull. It was said to have been blown up by a bomb planted by the page of a MacLean wife who was jealous of her husband's interest in a Spanish lady on board. Sir Lachlan MacLean and his Spanish party 'accompanyed with a grite nawmer

of thevis broken men, and sornars of Clannis, besydid the nawmer of ane hundred Spanyeartis come, bodin in fear of weir, to his Majesteis proper ilis of Canna Rum Eg and the Isle of Elennole (Muck), and after they had scorned, wracked and spolled the saidis hail Illis, they treassonablie raised fyre and in maist barborous, shameful and cruell maner, brynt the same Illis, with the haill men, weimen and childrene being thairintill, not spairing the pupullis and infantis . . . the like barbarous and shameful crueltie has sendle been herd of amagis Chriseanis in ony kingdome of age.'

The interesting aspect of this case is that when complaints were raised, they were made not by Clanranald but by the King's Advocate, and Mac-Lean was not incriminated for his desecration of the people but the fact that he had employed Spaniards, enemies of the King, in a private war against his subjects. MacLean was imprisoned in Edinburgh Castle but, allowed out on bail, made his escape aided, it is thought, by Queen Elizabeth and James VI. They turned a blind eye to his deeds because it helped weaken the MacDonalds during this time, described by George Thompson, in his *Antiquity of the Christian Religion amongst the Scots*, as being 'so on fire with civil wars, so polluted with massacre and bloodshed, that nought else seemed to exist but a perpetual shambles'.

Eigg is depicted at this time as being 'ane Ile verie fertile and commodious baith for all kinds of bestiall and corns, specialle aittis for eftir everie boll of aittis sawing in the same ony yeair will grow 10 or 12 bollis agane. It is 30 merk land, and it perteins to the Clan Ranald, and will raise 60 men to the weiris'. All these men were mustered during Sir James MacDonald's rebellion against the Crown. In 1615 Sir James disputed the power of the Argylls over territory in Islay he alleged belonged to him. Sir James hated the Argylls whom he characterised as a race that 'craves ever to fish in drumlie [muddy] waters' and repeatedly declared that he would die sooner than see them possess Islay. He was imprisoned in Edinburgh for 'treasonous activities' but escaped. A reward of £2,000 was offered for him dead or alive but, with the aid of fellow islanders, he made his way to Sleat and from there sailed, with a party, 'in a large boat' to Eigg. Here they joined Coll Mac-Gillespick who was also feuding with the Argylls. Sir James MacDonald was enthusiastically received by his clansmen on Eigg. 'He and those who had come with him stood in a place by themselves, whilst Coll MacGillespick's men marched round them, firing volleys of small arms for half an hour; and afterwards every individual came forward and shook hands with the chief'. According to the historian Gregory, the army, now 300 strong, slaughtered cattle to ensure a supply of provisions and sailed south to Argyll. The Privy Council were 'not idle in taking steps to repress this insurrection' but their efforts were hampered by the absence of the Earl of Argyll who 'being much pressed by his numerous creditors, had lately gone to England, without any prospect of immediate return'. The government raised the price on Sir James's head to £5,000, put one on Coll MacGillespick and several others of their followers and tried to rally support from mainland chiefs loyal to the Crown 'to pursue the rebels by sea'.

On the 18th June Sir James arrived at Isle of Colonsay, where more cattle were killed for provisions, and four or five days later landed on Islay where his army ambushed and occupied the Castle of Dunyveg. The rebels then moved on to Kintyre where Sir James sent the 'firey cross through the district' summoning all Argyll's vassals to come and take new charters from him and was 'very gladly received' by many of the Kintyre men. On 16th August, Argyll, eventually persuaded to return home, was given 400 soldiers and supplies by the Crown. Sir James's forces now numbered nearly 1,000 men but even so, tactical manoeuvres and good spy work allowed Argyll to make a suprise attack on his camp. Sir James 'perceiving his followers to be much disordered, forsook his camp and took flight'. He re-grouped at Islay but it was of no avail and he fled, along with many of his chiefs, first to Ireland and then to Spain while Coll MacGillespick surrendered upon 'assurance of his own life and the lives of some few of his followers'. The Crown was delighted at the departure of so many chiefs, realising that 'so long as the heads are all to the fore, the rebellion will never be thought quenched' and, indeed, it was the last attempt by a MacDonald to recapture the position of Lord of the Isles. It was also the end of an era endorsed by the fact that, in 1613, Ian, heir to the chiefship of Clanranald, had married Marion, daughter of Sir Rory MacLeod of Dunvegan, so bringing their feud to a close.

CHURCH AND STATE

The Reformation happened a hundred years later in Scotland. It was not until 1560 that the ethos of Calvinism preached by John Knox became the religious rule, the practice of the Catholic Mass was made punishable by death and priests were officially banished. However, on the remote islands, the 'Paroch kirk' continued with its services, partly because no Protestant minister was sent to replace the resident Catholic priest and partly because many chiefs, including the Clanranalds, remained adherents of the old faith as a way of continuing to claim independence from the Crown. John Moydartch, captain of Clanranald, even built a new church at Kildonnan in the second half of the 16th century. During his life he was involved in many conflicts and the church was one of seven he was told to build, or repair, as penance for his various misdeeds.

The church, a massive structure of local stone and lime rubble, stands on the supposed site of St Donnan's old building. Today it is a ruin but certain features remain; a lintel window at the east end, a tomb recess in the north wall with two free stone panels, the top one dated 1641 and initialled 'DR' and the lower bearing the Clanranald arms. On the west wall there was a crudely carved head

Cathedral Cave

of an angel, which has now been removed, and on the floor two grave slabs exist with incised crosses. A tomb is said to contain the bones of Ranald MacDonald, the famous 18th-century piper. In the graveyard there is the shaft of a 15th-century cross with a modern top. It is the last of a line erected to guide pilgrims to St Donnan's church. From one cross the next was visible, making a chain of stations.

After the Reformation the church fell into disrepair and illicit services were held on Eigg in the Cathedral Cave, *Uamh Chrabhaiche*, on the south-west side of the island. Its yawning interior is curtained by a steady stream of drips from the hillside above and measures 255 feet long by 30 feet wide and is 60 feet high. A ledge of rock, half-way up the left-hand side, acted as the altar and pulpit and the dank, ghoulish aura of the place prompted Sir Walter Scott, on a visit in the 19th century, to write that 'the appearance of a priest and Highland congregation in such an extraordinary place of worship, might have engaged the pencil of Salvator'. The cave is cut off by the sea at high tide, a fact which made one islander irreverently remark that 'It must have meant the sermons could not continue for too long'.

In 1609 the island chiefs were forced to sign the Statutes of Iona and accept its terms which included the rebuilding of ruinous churches, acceptance of Calvinistic traditions and a limit to the size of their households. There was a move to make them speak English for Gaelic was the language spoken in Catholic areas and English in Protestant ones. Bards, who were the holders of Gaelic culture, were not to be received on the islands and gentlemen, or yeomen, worth sixty cows or more must send their eldest son to the Lowlands to be educated in English.

By the beginning of the 17th century there were no priests left in the Highlands and Islands and appeals for help were answered by an Irish Franciscan College, founded at Louvain in 1606 by Philip II of Spain, to keep alive Gaelic Catholic culture and learning during these dark days. Father McCann arrived in the islands in 1619 but was arrested and banished in 1622 when the first Protestant minister was appointed. Neil MacKinnon was attached to Sleat on Skye but his parish extended over the whole of the Small Isles. An enormous and ungovernable area for one man and, in 1624, its defences were breached by Father Cornelius Ward who landed on Eigg in August the following year. He found the church at Kildonnan roofless and that the people had forgotten the rituals of the Mass. The people of Eigg made him swear on the sacred missal that his words were the truth and at the end of eight days' preaching 'two only short of 200 exchanged their heresy for the Faith'. One of the people who abstained was related to Neil MacKinnon and probably alerted him to the events on Eigg because he subsequently led a night raid 'with soldiers' against his rival in religion. However, he was persuaded by his friends not to seize Ward and further persuaded by Clanranald to stay off the island and leave the Catholics in peace with the inducement of the teinds of a third of the island.

Father Ward went to Rhum from Eigg, where he retrieved seventeen people from the Protestant faith, and from there to Canna where he was horrified to discover they 'paid more attention to the harvest than their own souls'. The Clanranald gave Father Ward his full support in his mission and on 5th February, 1626, he took the unusual step of writing to Pope Urban VIII in gratitude for sending the Franciscan and 'redeeming and enlightening our people who for this long time have sat in darkness'.

Father Ward was captured in London in 1629 but his mission was continued by Father Patrick Hegerty who toured the Small Isles in 1630. He visited Muck on 10th August where he 'converted' three persons and christened two before being chased by the Calvinists to Eigg. Here he made one hundred converts, christened twelve, celebrated twelve marriages and heard many confessions. After a short visit to Moidart he again returned to Eigg and in four days took twelve more into the church, married two others and travelled on to other islands. Then, in April 1631, he was warned that Bishop Knox was planning his arrest and fled to Ireland. Father Hegerty was the last priest the islanders saw before Father Dermit Dugan arrived in 1652. His reports show scant knowledge of the Franciscan missions, indicating the secrecy with which they were carried out and the firmness with which their teachings were suppressed, because Father Hegerty believed the revival of Catholicism was solely due to his efforts. He proudly claimed to convert '800–900' souls on Eigg, Canna and other islands where 'scarce 15 . . . knew any of the mysteries of our holy Faith . . . persons of 70, 80, 100 or even 120 years of age had never received holy baptism'.

Father Dugan's work, and that of other Catholic missionaries during the 17th century, was constantly undermined by the growing power of the protestant Earls of Argyll. In 1627 they secured the superiority of Eigg from the protestant Bishop of the Isles. This, in effect, transferred church land to private ownership and put the Argylls in a position to choose their own tenants and demand rent. In addition the Crown, still unable to control the Hebrides from the seat of government in Edinburgh, began using the Argylls as their agents. The Argylls' wealth and power increased while the chiefs, with the feudal system of ownership over, their source of money gone, and rent demanded for their own land, fell into a state of accelerating debt partly incurred by their changing situation. Closer contact between James VI and the island chiefs brought new financial commitments. The MacDonalds of Sleat had to pay 10,000 merks each as security that they would keep the peace and find 5,000 merks to finance their feu duty and annual appearance before the Privy Council. This trip was very expensive; the distance to be travelled, the neglect of business while away, lawyers bills, and agents who had to be paid. There was also their new lifestyle to be maintained which required smart clothes. Clanranald's accounts contain a bill of over £700 for expensive cloth, lace, French ribbon and silver buttons bought from an Edinburgh merchant, George Graham. It is dated 1669 which was a time when he was in considerable financial trouble.

Attempts to right this state of affairs were made by chiefs leasing 'wadsets' (mortgages) of land usually granted for quite large sums of money. The Clanranald wadset his lands in Eigg, Uist and on the mainland to MacDonald of Sleat for amounts varying from 1,000 to 27,000 merks. In 1633 he granted the wadset of Moidart, Arisaig and further land on South Uist to Lord Lorne, son of the Duke of Argyll, for £26,000. Earlier that year Clanranald had granted a commission to the Earl of Seaforth to collect money owing on his land 'for the reliefing of his burdines and debtis resting to us and utheris'. His difficulties continued and in 1700 he owed MacDonald of Sleat £64,000, who was also deeply in debt to the tune of 100,000 merks. Even so, few estates changed hands or broke up during the 17th century largely due to the loyalty of kinsmen and vassals who took up a large number of wadsets.

The Argylls exploited the chief's weakness to their own ends, while they supported any cause which attempted to check Argyll power. Unfortunately, the Clanranalds constantly backed the losers and these campaigns cost them more money. When, in 1642, Charles I declared war against Cromwell and his Parliament and commissioned Montrose to raise an army in Scotland, the Clanranalds, as vassals of Argyll, should have joined his covenanting forces. Instead they supported Montrose, raised the men of Eigg, Uist, Moidart and Arisaig, raided Sunart for its sheep and cattle to feed their garrisons and marched to Montrose's camp at Mingarry. Here 'they were joyfully and gladly welcomed by Montrose and all the rest'. Throughout the campaign the Clanranalds withheld their rents from Argyll but, in May 1650, the Synod of Argyll ordered the presbytery of Skye 'to use every dilligence in collecting the stipends of the vacant churches in Clanranald's bounds which, in South Uist alone, amounted to 4,900 merks (£3,266)'.

In 1651 the Clanranalds were excommunicated and made social, political and religious outcasts. This action perhaps brought them to some form of obedience for, in 1680, Argyll declared that he would not press Clanranald for his debts on account of 'the good services done and performed to us by the said Captaine'. In 1685 the Clanranalds were forced to fight with Argyll in his unsuccessful rising to uphold Monmouth's rebellion. When the 9th Earl of Argyll was executed for his treason the Clanranalds, hoping for delivery from their services, swiftly changed sides, supporting James VI in his fight against the protestant Covenanters. However, when Argyll's son returned from exile in Holland with William and Mary, his father's forfeiture was reversed and all his vassals were once more sub-ject to his power. James VI fled the country and left his defenders to meet their reprisals.

The consequences of the 1688 Revolution which established the Presbyterian Church of Scotland were foretold by an Eigg seer. In 1685 he addressed Father O'Rain's mass at Kildonnan with the words, 'They should all flit . . . people of strange and different habits and arms were to come . . . to use all acts of hostility, as killing, burning, tirling and deforcing of women . . . [He had] seen an apparition of a man in a red coat lined with blue and . . . a strange sort of blue cap with a very high cock . . . kissing a comely maid of Kildonnan . . . a man in such a dress would certainly debauch . . . such a young woman.' A few families took heed of his warning and left. The prophecy was borne out when, in 1689, Major James Ferguson was sent north with six hundred men in two ships, the *Lamb* and the *Dartmouth*, to 'overawe the adherents of the exiled James II'. They landed at Tiree where one, John Fraser, was removed for his Episcopalian tendencies and then put in at Armadale on Skye where a Cameronian was killed in a brawl with a boat crew from Eigg who happened also to be there. The *Dartmouth* then sailed for Eigg where the Cameronians landed in their red coats lined with blue, and high-cocked hats. Ferguson wreaked revenge on the islanders and, true to the prophecy, a Kildonnan girl was raped but 'her misfortune being pitied, and not reckoned her crime' she was forgiven and later married an islander.

In an effort to stamp out further insurrections various repressive measures were taken against the Highlands. One was the increased suppression of the Gaelic language. Rents were granted to the Synod of Argyll to erect English schools 'for rooting out the Irish language, and other pious

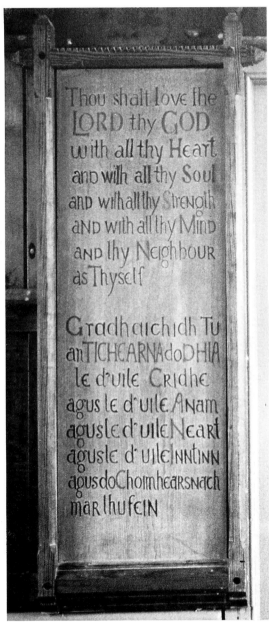

Panels in the Church of Scotland

uses'. Then, an Act was passed in 1696 which placed the financing of the new schools upon the chiefs and their principal tenants. Opposition to this policy drew together Highlanders of every religion and, to counter this, a number of wealthy people in south Scotland banded together in 1709, under the title of The Society in Scotland for Propagating Christian Knowledge, to provide charity schools in the Highlands and Islands. The schools were to be manned by teachers of proven loyalty to teach the English language, the Presbyterian Calvinist religion, church music and arithmetic only and criticisms of the banning of Gaelic in the politico-religious schools were brushed aside.

The Act of Union between Scotland and England was passed in 1707 and this 'unequal incorporating Union' led to the Jacobite Rising of 1715. The men of Eigg and the other islands rallied behind the Clanranald, wearing a sprig of white heather 'whereby they might be known as they had not military habit or livery' and shouting their own individual war-cry. At the battle of Sherrifmuir the Clanranald was killed, shot by a silver bullet. It was believed that the Clanranalds could not be killed by lead and the chief was so sure of his immunity that he wore red for the battle. Nevertheless, it is said, that a man from Moidart, who had enlisted as an alternative to being punished for theft, knew of the claim and loaded his gun with a silver bullet.

The Rising was suppressed and George I and Scottish Presbyterians persisted with their policies. Eigg became a refuge for Catholics from neighbouring islands. When the protestant MacLean of Coll acquired Rhum in 1725 he insisted the inhabitants change their religion. Protestantism became known as the 'Faith of the Yellow Stick' because, the story goes, MacLean used to bar the islanders' route to church with a yellow stick which they were forced to grip and swear they would change their religion. The Clanranald gave many Catholics who refused, land on Eigg, and the MacQuarries are one family who can trace their origins back to this event.

A schoolmaster, James Wright, was despatched to the Small Isles on 23 May, 1728, as part of the SPCK's continued efforts at conversion. Later that year the Committee's Minutes record a letter from Dr Donald MacQueen, who had been appointed Minister of Sleat and the Small Isles in 1727, 'shewing that he visits the School frequently, and finds some of the schollars advance but slowly, being often taken from the school on account of the poverty of their parents, others read the scriptures and others books tollerably, are writing, do repeat the Catechism and a part of the Protestants Resolution, that the Master reads, prays and sings Psalms with the people on the Lord's Day in his absence'. Poverty was the common lot and in bad years it was 'the use and wont' of chiefs to remit tenants' rents and supply them with grain. The welfare of the clan still largely depended on the chief who was regarded as their mediator and Prince. A report to the Government in 1721 stated that, in spite of all measures taken, the chief was the Highlanders' idol and that they had 'an inherent attractive virtue which makes their people follow as iron clamps to the loadstone'.

They followed when the Clanranalds supported Prince Charles Edward's claim to the Scottish throne. The people of Eigg rallied to the heroic songs composed by the famous Gaelic bard, Alexander MacDonald, who lived on Eigg. ·A great bard with patriotic views and stirring words was a force to be reckoned with and the Clanranalds owe much of their glory to songs such as this:

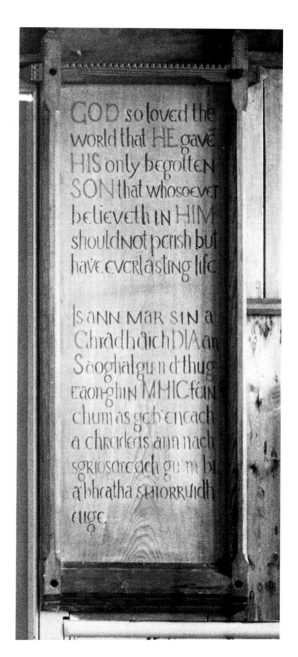

My treasure, my treasure, Clanranald,
Stag among the deer of the bens,
Salmon among the trout of the streams,
Loveliest among the swans,
Loftiest ship that makes the harbour.

The men of Eigg responded to the sentiments expressed in this Jacobite Rising Song.

Who, who, who will come with me across the
    mountains of Moidart?
Who, who, who will come with me across the
    mountains of Moidart?
Haste ye, make ye no delay.
The King of Dul will steer ye, [King of the Elements]
Haste ye, haste ye, Haste to come
For our King has landed in Moidart.

They were led by Ranald, son of the 17th Chief of Clanranald, because his father, fortunately it transpired, was too old and 'given to the bottle' to take part. Ranald joined the chiefs who met Charles Edward when he landed at Glenfinnan on 6th August, 1745. Prince Charles Edward's voyage on the French frigate, *Du Teillay*, took him round the south coast of Eigg and the contingent from the island was led by John Mac-Donald of Laig. They marched south in pursuit of the Jacobite cause and restoration of their freedom from English rule. It was not to be. Scottish support was patchy but, spurred on by an initial success at Prestonpans, they pressed on south to Derby where the Prince lost heart and withdrew until he was finally defeated by Cumberland at the Battle of Culloden. The Prince considered regrouping and planned a headquarters on Eigg but, in the event, he escaped back to France while, in Scotland, Cumberland set about earning his nickname of 'the Butcher'.

Because the 'Old Clanranald' had not fought in the Rising and because of an arrangement made in 1726 whereby he was, in fact, only the life-renter of his estates from the Argylls – to which his son was the outright owner – the Clanranald estates were not forfeited, although they were included in a Covenanters' survey. The young Clanranald took refuge on Eigg until he was able to reach the mainland and join many other Highland chiefs who later took refuge in France. He hid in a cave now called Clanranald's cave, *Uamha Mhic 'ic Ailein*, situated at the lonely north end of Eigg. Here Clanranald spent several days eating his meals, it is said, off a stone in the cave with a broad table-like top and attended by his batman from Uist named John MacLellan. On his first night Clanranald instructed MacLellan to prepare him a bed. MacLellan could only find a stone to serve as a pillow but Clanranald, seeing this, asked if he could not get something more comfortable such as a turf. His batman, it is reported, was scathing in his reply announcing, 'How fond you are of ease. Will the stone not suffice the head you may lose before morning'.

Thirty-eight men from Eigg survived the battle of Culloden, including John MacDonald of Laig, and they returned to the island. A year later the Government dispatched a party of ships to rout out rebels on the islands and meet reprisals. Eigg was visited by Captain Duff and Captain John Ferguson on their ships the HMS *Commodore* and *Furnace* in May and one hundred men were sent ashore to collect arms. Few emerged and a search was ordered by the protestant minister, Donald MacQueen. He advised John MacDonald to surrender and promised him clemency and also persuaded him to send for the rest of the men and their arms. Some dozen men appeared whereupon Ferguson ordered MacDonald to be seized, stripped him of his clothes and claimed to find a piece of paper 'containing a list of all the Eigg folk, that were in the Prince's service'. These men were 'snatched aboard' and, since most of them were married, they left a 'throng of families'. Among them were 'Angus M'Donald, farmer at Grulin: John M'Donald, farmer at Howlin: Roderick M'Donald, farmer at Kirktown: John M'Dougall, pedlar of Galnashel: John M'Lean, gardener at Laagg: Donald M'Donald, farmer at Fivepenny, taken upon suspicion but never was in the Rebellion'. They were all transported.

Captain Ferguson then proceeded to slaughter cattle, burn houses and ravish 'a girl or two' before sailing for Tobermory where the prisoners were transferred to a tender. On 15th June Ferguson returned to Eigg, perhaps because he had heard of Prince Charles's idea of setting up a headquarters on the island, but finding nothing, went on to Canna. Prince Charles in fact left Loch nam Uamh for France on the 20th September but so secretly that, during November, some French privateers landed on Eigg hoping to rescue him but were told he had fled.

The men from Eigg were transported to hulks at Inverness or, some say, the Thames. Those still alive were tried and two were released, among them Captain MacDonald who returned to Kinlochmoidart. The rest were taken to Barbados where they spent the rest of their lives.

John MacLellan, Clanranald's batman, was a survivor and parted from his master on good terms because he was awarded the farm of Sandavore for his services. MacLellan refused this saying it was a 'scrappy, useless place' and that he would rather have grazing at Kildonnan which he got with a cottage. He was also eligible for the 1/- a year pension given to supporters. This had to be collected from Edinburgh and MacLellan used to make the journey on foot. One year he happened to pass through a farm in Perthshire where the farmer and his men were busy at the harvest.

Because it was so soon after Culloden MacLellan felt uncertain of the reception he might meet and hid in a concealed place but, even so, was seen by one of the workers. MacLellan asked for the farmer and was directed to a middle-aged man who was lame. The farmer received him most cordially and when MacLellan asked him why he was lame replied that he was out during the 1745 campaign, on the government side, and had received a severe wound at the battle of Falkirk. He would have died had it not been for the kind act of one of the enemy who lifted him from the battlefield and laid him beside a wall out of harm's way. 'Well,' said MacLellan 'I was the man who lifted you'. The farmer then, needless to say, treated him with great kindness and hospitality.

In his later days MacLellan became a notorious drunkard and was a regular customer at the mill which, in those days, also acted as a change house for illegally distilled whisky. One night, when tottering home intoxicated past the cemetery at Kildonnan, MacLellan imagined that the dead were out quarrelling amongst themselves and admonished them to be on their best behaviour or he would go up and 'leather them with his stick'.

A TIME OF CHANGE

The Scots way of life began to change after the Union with England in 1707. These alterations accelerated after the Jacobite Rising in 1745. Increased contact with the progressive south had a dramatic effect on industry and agriculture particularly in the Lowlands and Central Scotland. The British Government continued their attempts to break the clan system by curbing their powers with restrictive measures and encouraging their chiefs to move south. Many did, and discovered other occupations and entertainments. They became absentee landlords more interested in the rents their tenants could provide to support their new way of life, than their welfare.

The Clanranalds, whose rights had not been removed after Culloden, were slower than most to forsake their traditional way of life. Captain Burt, visiting the Isles in the 18th century, expressed surprise that 'all the clansmen were entertained in the hall of their chief, although strictly according to their degree. The chief's piper and fiddler made music for them. The weddings and funerals of members of the chief's family were events for the whole clan. Everyone joined the party'. Another traveller, named Stanhope, who accompanied Lord MacDonald on his progress through Skye, said that 'no king could command the homage, veneration and service which, wherever he trod, was his undisputed right'. When the chiefs ceased to live among their people, Captain Burt noted, 'they became soured' while others expressed the view that, with the break-up of the clans, the character of the people changed; they lost much of their former frankness and ease of manner.

But a standard of behaviour and kinship survived, based on the old society where everyone carried arms, giving them their pride in descent, pioneering and soldierly qualities, breeding and fine manners and a *savoir-faire* remarked on by many outsiders. In former times a large population of potential warriors was encouraged to live off a small area of land as the general lawlessness of the country made it expedient for chiefs to maintain as many followers as possible. To this end holdings were divided and subdivided because, as William Marshall wrote in 1793, 'A good soldier or a fool-hardy desperado was of more value than a good husbandman'. Farms were frittered down and the country 'burdened with a load of tenantry'. There was a widespread and ancient belief that long occupation gave you a right, or 'kindness', over land probably dating back to the old Celtic system where everything belonged to everyone and the destruction of the clans was bitterly resented.

At the end of the 18th century Eigg was heavily populated. A survey was made for the first time. It was conducted by the Revd. John Walker between 1764 and 1771 and he lists the population as:

1. Eigg among 459 Inhabitants contains a Man of 80, a Woman of 85, and another of 89.

2. The Males are 183 and the Females 276.

3. It contains 110 Fencible Men, from 16 to 60 that is one forth and 19/110 of the whole Inhabitants.

4. The Number of Families are 88. So that the Families contain at an Average 5 19/21 Persons. Of these Families, the least Numerous consists of two Persons, of which there are 8 upon the Island and there are only 3 Families which contain 9, 10 and 11 Persons.

5. In 10 Families, in Eigg there is no Marriage, In the remaining 78 Families, there is a Marriage in each; and the Number of Children in these Families is 186, that is 2 30/78 Children to each Marriage (225).

These people lived a primitive life, according to the entry on Eigg written by the Minister, the Revd. Donald MacLean, in the *Statistical Account of Scotland*. This was prepared for the great agricultural reformer, Sir John Sinclair, between 1791 and 1799 and it was the first time that anyone had bothered to properly evaluate the exact state of the country.

The Revd. MacLean describes the land of Eigg as being 'equally divided between crops and pasture ground' and in good seasons maintains, albeit in a 'scanty' way, its present population. They grew barley, oats, potatoes, flax, kails and a few 'garden stuffs'. A quarter of the land was ploughed and the rest dug with a spade. The land was manured with seaweed. In bad years meal was imported and in good, potatoes, butter and cheese were exported. Seed time began about the 1st of April and harvest around 12th September although, in 1793, 'the crop was not got in until near the end of November'. Most had enough grazing for two 'horned cattle' and their followers. The parish contained about 1,100 cows; 540 stirks and 500 two-year-olds. It was a perennial difficulty getting them to sale because of the 'great distance from public markets, both by land and water. This circumstance renders it necessary to sell their cattle to private dealers, who in general think it their interest, to appreciate advantages arising from the local situation'. The people also kept horses, sheep and a few goats. They made oil from the blubber of seals and trapped otters for their fur which was sold 'at a price proportionate to its size'.

There were plentiful supplies of fish, the principal kinds caught being herrings, cod and ling but because 'the islanders had few fishing materials they seldom got a competency for their own families'. Ling must have been the exception for they were exported, fetching £31 to £31.10s for every '20 in the Clyde market'. Salt for curing had to be imported and the punitive tax put it out of range of the 'lower class, who are the bulk of the people' and created an illicit trade. The oil from the liver of the 'Cerban or Sun fish' was also extracted and exported.

Their diet was supplemented by sea birds, especially the shearwater and puffin. Large numbers inhabited the cliffs stretching from Laig to the east side of the island. They made their burrows in the cliff tops and the young 'before they leave the nest, are as large as the dam, trans-

parent with fat, and delicious to the taste of many' and were trapped.

The people lived in primitive, thatched houses built of dry stone with a central fire fuelled by peat and heath of which 'there was a competency'. Their dress was changing; formerly the men wore a belted plaid, short jacket, philibeg, bonnet and tartan 'shore hose' but latterly short jackets, long trousers and hats had come into fashion which were found to be 'far more convenient'. The new styles were introduced by men 'drafted to the American War or seafaring visitors'. The women wore short and long cloaks, great coats and ribbands. The white 'kerchief', formerly worn by all married women to signify their status, had fallen out of use. This change is attributed to young women who went to the low country for the harvest. The money they earned, MacLean complains, was entirely spent on clothes. 'They seldom bring home any share of the price of their labour in cash, and they are a means of encouraging extravagance of dress'.

Besides farming and fishing many of the people practised other trades. There were '8 male and 6 female weavers, 1 house-carpenter, and 5 boat-carpenters, 5 taylors, and 2 smiths . . . two merchants, who bring their goods from the Glasgow market. There is one clergyman of the Established church, one Roman Catholic priest, one surgeon, and one schoolmaster; all these have their residence in Eigg'.

Food to feed their 'numerous family of weak children' seems to have been the prime consideration of most islanders, whereas that of money was in the forefront of Clanranald's mind. In 1763 he built a mill on Sandavaig burn and stipulated that the tenants of the larger farms and the islanders use it to grind their corn. The islanders, needless to say, resented this intrusion and extra expense but the proprietor was obdurate and the miller sent round the crofters' houses to destroy their querns. Local knowledge made him avoid one or two households where the 'tenants were hefty fellows' as he guessed it 'wouldn't be difficult to know him the next morning'.

The first miller was Angus MacDonald and he was succeeded by Alistair Mackay, who lived at Brae Cottage situated in the steep glade above Kildonnan. Alistair's father, Charlie Mor, was a notorious sheep stealer who lived at Arisaig. He was caught and deported to Coll where he soon resumed his nefarious trade and was then evicted to Muck. Again he proved a 'bad tenant' and the landlord's agent sent him packing. Charlie Mor then crossed to Eigg where he became the scourge of the miller's family. For a while he lived in a primitive dwelling under the lee of a big rock, covered with a tarpaulin, but later had the idea of converting some ruins near the mill into a house for himself and his two daughters, Jean and Catherine. However, Alistair wanted nothing to do with 'the old rogue' and whatever his father built during the day he demolished at night. Eventually Alistair became tired of this conflict and asked everyone on the island, including the minister, to come to the mill and discuss the problem. It was decided to build Charlie Mor a small house a quarter of a mile along the shore from the mill. Here the old fellow ended his days tended by his daughters who were not on the best of terms and 'it was no uncommon sight to see the two of them on fine moonlight nights fighting on the sands'.

Another story told about the renegade, Charlie Mor, is that one day, when he was out fishing on the rocks at the end of Castle Island, he saw a lobster in a crevice and forced his hand in to catch it where it stuck. The tide was flowing and, when the water reached his shoulders, Charlie realised the inevitable outcome and, taking his knife, prepared to cut off his hand when, with one final effort, he managed to extricate it but 'left all the skin of his hand on the rock and rowed his dingy home with his hand a mess of raw flesh and blood'.

Building Charlie Mor a house did not end the aggravation he caused his son. Eventually his family persuaded him to emigrate to America as they could not tolerate the old man's visits 'reminding them almost daily that supposing their heads reached the highest Heavens' he was still their grandfather. 'A fact which they resented and would gladly like to forget.' The Miller was not the first to emigrate. Between 1788 and 1790 many people left the Small Isles; 183 going to America and 55 to the mainland and neighbouring islands. 176 people left Eigg. 'A principal cause of this emigration was that the country was overstocked with people arising from frequent early marriages; of course the lands were able to supply them, but scantily, with the necessaries of life. It is not infrequent, upon these occasions, for a parent to divide with his newly married son the pittance of land (sometimes a very small portion of a farm) possessed by him, which must reduce both to poverty and misery.' But an added cause was the 'land of Eigg, which was formerly in part rented by small tenants, was divided among 8 principal tenants'.

As the Industrial Revolution gained momentum in the south and towns could no longer provide their own food, a large demand grew for imported meat. Prices rose for cattle and also for sheep with the highest amounts given for the big, prolific Blackface and Cheviot breeds developed in the Borders. Some of these sheep reached Eigg in 1791 and began to displace the islanders' small Shetland-type breed which had fine fleeces, little flesh and, because they were milked for human consumption, often only lambed every second year. It was estimated by Sir John Sinclair that an acre worth 2½d under cattle brought in 2s with sheep and these rises accelerated with the scarcities produced by the Napoleonic War. As prices increased so did the need for land and rents trebled.

Until the end of the 18th century Eigg was held 'in tack' by a relative of the Clanranalds based at Boisdale on South Uist. This meant that a chief with expanding lands gave a holding to a favourite son or relative in return for money which could take the form of an annual 'feu' or a lump sum called a 'wadset'. Sometimes these bequests were permanent but more often the land was let on long leases which might last a lifetime. The leasers were called 'tacksmen' and they, in turn, let most of their land to sub-tenants. The system became integral to the agriculture of the Highlands.

In early times sub-tenants paid for their land with labour dues but, by the end of the 16th century, these were largely commuted into rents payable in money and kind under a complicated arrangement which depended on the clan spirit. According to Mrs Grant, writing in the 18th century, 'All the intercourse of life was carried on by a kind of tacit agreement and interchange of good offices that would appear extravagant elsewhere

The Old Mill

. . . The ground being all unenclosed, it depended entirely on the good faith and herding of his neighbour, whether a man ever put a sheaf in his barn . . . The sheep and cattle too, wandering promiscuously on the hills, the integrity of a man's neighbour was all that he had to depend on for their return'.

All the fertile land on Eigg, as in most parts of the Highlands, is limited to the hill slopes and raised beaches along the seashore. This land was jointly cultivated and divided into areas of 'in-field' and 'out-field', the proportion varying according to the lie of the land. The 'in-field', as the name suggests, was nearer to the houses for ease of working. This type of farming was called 'run-rig', the term coming, it is thought, from the Gaelic *Roinn-ruith* meaning 'division run'. The fields were described as looking all interwoven 'like a piece of striped cloth with banks full of weeds and ridges of corn in constant succession'. The parallel ridges of the old run-rigs can be discerned on Eigg north of the Cleadale crofts,

The land at Cleadale

above Laig Farm and at Grulin in areas which have remained upploughed since 1810.

The in-field was usually the best land, under constant cultivation and given all the available manure. Only a portion of the out-field was used, until its fertility was exhausted, and it was manured by folding the animals over it. In addition each farmer had rights to common grazing. The change from communal farms to crofts altered the landscape. Instead of it being patterned with holdings in common fields there were small stone enclosures for individual arable farms with communal grazing only in selected areas. Most of the crofts on Eigg had three to four acres of arable ground and common grazing rights for about three cows and their progeny, the size of a croft being measured by the amount of stock it was allowed on the common grazing.

The new commercial farms supported a far smaller population and many landlords encouraged emigration. Initially government policy discouraged emigration because the area was an important recruiting pool for the Highland regiments. Press gangs were active on Eigg; several islanders served under Wellington in the Peninsular war and the population fell from 500 to 442 between 1801 and 1811. Men with families were exempt from military service and island boys began marrying at sixteen.

A Macdonald from Sleat called Domhall Gorm was in charge of the Press Gang. He took four sons from one widow on Eigg and she cursed his name. Domhall Gorm went to Spain in command of the young men and one day, when they were drawn up in battle order, Domhall, in a fine humour, boasted that he was thriving on the widow's curses. 'No sooner had he uttered the words than he was killed by a shot from a French battery'. Findlay MacCormick of Grulin nobly took the place of another widow's only son who was being pressed into the army. Nothing more was heard of him until, many years later, an islander met a man from Sleat at the market in Skye. He said that Findlay had fought alongside him against the French but had been wounded and, as he could not keep up with the rest of the army, had been made comfortable and left in a hut. It was the last news of Findlay to ever reach Eigg.

Prices for kelp then began to rise and the Clanranald discouraged emigration, needing workers to gather in the seaweed. Many small tenants who had previously paid their rent from the proceeds of cattle now began to use kelp. On Eigg the seaweed had always been gathered but it was mainly used for manure. The Laig shore was divided between the crofters and the MacDonald at Laig farm and there were specific laws relating to the distribution of the seaweed. Anyone noticing a large bulk washed ashore, as usually happened after stormy weather, had to send word round Cleadale and all the members of the township descended to the beach to salvage as much as possible. But if anyone began to carry the seaweed to his own croft without telling the rest, he would be deprived of what he had already salvaged and only given his fair share.

Seaweed entered the mythology of the Western Isles. Stories emerged, which have their counterparts in Greece, of figures bound to the rocks by the weed and that rooted to rocks and floating at high-tide on the surface of the sea is the hair of drowned women. They made up songs to sing as they worked pulling in the seaweed with narrow hay-forks, tossing it ashore, collecting it in carts and stacking it in a dry place. This one was collected on Eigg by Kenneth MacLeod.

PULLING THE SEA DULSE

A-do, A-de.

Clings dulse to the sea-rock,
Clings heart to the loved one,
Be't high tide or low tide,
A-do, A-de.

Pulling the dulse by the sea-rocks at low tide,
Ne'er pull I thy love, lad,
Be't high tide or low,
A-do, A-de.

Clings dulse to the sea-rock
Clings heart to the loved one,
Be't high tide or low tide,
A-do, A-de, A-de.

Shoreward the sea-mew comes flying at low tide,
But seaward my heart flies out seaward to thee,
A-do, A-de.

Clings dulse to the sea-rock
Clings heart to the loved one,
Be't high tide or low tide,
A-do, A-de.

The Singing Sands with Rhum in the distance

By 1811 *Accounts* mention that 'Considerable quantities of kelp are made on Eigg, especially on the western side where there is a beautiful semi-amphitheatre fenced with a natural enclosure of rocks adapted to the cultivation of corn and the manufacture of kelp'. The beaches of Castle Island were also 'rich in seaweed' and made a 'finer kelp than could be made elsewhere in Eigg'. During low tide all the men, women and children worked on the shore until the incoming sea was over their knees. The seaweed was carted in creels to dry rocks, spread out until it putrified, put in kilns, set alight and allowed to burn for six to eight hours until the whole was reduced to a fused grey mass. Then it was carefully raked, sprinkled with sea-water and broken into convenient pieces. Twenty to twenty-two tons of seaweed were required to produce one ton of kelp. The ash, or kelp, was rich in alkali. The discovery is credited to one Rory MacDonald of North Uist who, in his first attempt, succeeded in reducing the seaweed to ashes and so gained the name of 'Rory, maker of ashes'. Kelp was used not only for bleaching linen, producing glass and soap but also for gun-powder. The Napoleonic wars stopped the importation of barilla, the alternative source of alkali, from Spain and the price of kelp leapt from £1 to £20 a ton and shores that attracted the 'golden fringe' became enormously valuable. The chiefs and tacksmen offered people land as inducements to come and work the seaweed which was seasonal work. Farms were sub-divided into even smaller holdings. Between 1808 and 1810 Reginald George MacDonald of Clanranald made £42,000 from kelp produced on Eigg and Canna. Fifteen to twenty thousand tons of kelp were exported annually from the Hebrides at this time and patterns of farming changed to allow time for the kelp harvest.

The industry collapsed at the end of the Napoleonic war and the price of kelp fell to £3 a ton. Many lairds were badly hit by the fall in income but their tenants were left destitute and their only alternative was starvation or emigration. The new small plots of land could not support the number of people now dependent on their produce. Even so they clung desperately to their homes and, in their increasing poverty, relied for subsistence on the potato. Clanranald introduced this tuber to the islands in 1739. He brought seed from his Irish estates and insisted it was planted in spite of island resistance to this novelty. When the crop was first lifted the people took the potatoes to him and declared that, although he might force them to grow such things, he could not make them eat them. However, they soon changed their minds when they saw the value of this hugely productive crop and by 1811 potatoes formed four-fifths of their food. Every inch of land was planted with potatoes in what were called 'lazy beds'. The term was a misnomer, for these long, narrow strips, separated by drainage ditches, were hard work to make with their primitive implements. Potatoes could also be produced with less effort than cereals during the summer months when every bit of available time was spent gathering kelp. The adverse effect was that crop rotation was abandoned and seaweed became too valuable for use as fertilizer. An added blow was that cattle prices also began to fall. The invention of the railway led to the demise of droving and newly-developed root crops allowed cattle to be kept on lowland farms.

Some lairds bankrupted themselves trying to provide for their starving people while others saw resettlement in America and the continued restocking of their land with sheep, whose mutton and wool were still fetching high prices, as the only solution.

TACKSMEN
AND TENANTS

In 1806 Reginald George Clanranald Esq. of Clanranald commissioned a detailed map of Eigg to be drawn by William Bald, a highly skilled surveyor and engineer, who made many fine maps of the north-west of Scotland. His map of Eigg shows it divided into ten townships, each consisting of a group of seven to fifteen scattered houses surrounded by strips of cultivated land. The island was densely populated at this time and every available piece of fertile ground was farmed. There are over 100 buildings marked, more than 1,000 acres of cultivated land, 1,000 of pasture, 3,500 of moor and 2.02 of loch totalling 5,685.80 acres. The ten main areas were: 'Upper and Lower Gruline, Galmisdale, Sandamore, Sandavore, Glebe, Kildonnan, Laig, Cleadale, Five Pennies and Houlaine'. Some of the land was farmed by tacksmen and some crofters. Stories of the more conspicuous inhabitants live on in the legends of Eigg.

Laig farmlands

LAIG

The principal farm was Laig, inhabited by the MacDonalds who were close relatives of the Clanranalds. The earliest record of their holding land here is contained in the *Book of Clanranald*. It mentions that, early in the 17th century, 'Allan, eldest son of Dugald VI of Clanranald, held lands at Morar of 14 Merklands and at Eigg of 9 Merklands' and further that on, 21st July, 1610, 'Allan bestowed on his son Alexander by charter land of Cnoc Oilteig'.

Laig farm, by 1806, amounted to 891.26 acres of which 79.55 were arable, 5.46 pasture and 806.25 consisted of moor. There were thirteen houses on the property lived in by, among others, two agricultural workers, one shepherd and a clergyman. The main house is the oldest of any size on the island. A solid, grey stone building, with an L-shaped extension added around 1930, it stands squarely above the southern end of Laig beach. The house has an underground escape tunnel leading from the dining room and out by the back door. No one knows where it ends but its existence was proved when, in 1923, one of the farm carts broke through into its hollow. An examination established that the tunnel was 3 feet broad but debris prevented the depth being measured.

The MacDonalds of Laig were a naturally flamboyant family and, as lairds of Eigg, their actions were watched by their tenants and servants, gossiped about, committed to memory and retold down the generations. Some stand out more than others. During the 18th century there was Ronald, who was a famous piper, and John, who led the men of Eigg in the Jacobite Rising. Another MacDonald, perhaps John's brother, was believed to have been killed at Culloden because he never returned and, since John was taken by Captain Ferguson during his reprisals, this was perhaps the reason why, in 1770, it is recorded that another Ronald MacDonald came to Eigg and took over the lease from the Clanranalds. He was the son of the celebrated Jacobite bard Alasdair mac Mahaighstir.

Ronald published a selection of his father's poems in 1776 and had two children, Angus and Mary. Angus inherited the farm on his father's death and married the daughter of Malcolm MacAskill of Kildonnan. He was a cultured man, genial host and, according to tradition, 'over fond of the bottle'. In 1812 the traveller, Necker de Saussure, visited Eigg and Laig farm and describes being shown the book of Gaelic poems and how they were written in 'peculiar characters, long since out of use'. Angus asked de Saussure's party to stay for dinner 'but before the cloth was laid, he made us drink a full glass of whiskey to the health of each'. The evening continued with much talk and song, de Saussure noting that 'When the old man mentioned the Campbells, we discovered . . . some traces of animosity. But . . . all the peers of the kingdom were nothing by the side of Clanranald, his chief . . . He diverted us greatly by singing some Gaelic songs; and . . . then sung some pibrochs . . . pleasingly imitating with his voice the sound of the bagpipe . . . On our departure, the good old Laig accompanied us to the door . . . Filling a glass with whiskey, he first drank himself, and then pouring out a bumper to each in succession, we emptied it . . . a very ancient custom denominated . . . *Deoch an Dorus*.'

Further evidence of Angus of Laig's devotion to the bottle comes out in another story. There was a gathering at the mill at Kildonnan which may have been after a funeral because the parish priest, Father Anthony MacDonald, was present. The party got rather rowdy as the drams were 'frequent and generous' and the hotelier complained about their behaviour. As Angus was the ring-leader the priest rebuked him but Angus, 'directly descended as he was from the line of Clanranald, and the blood running so proud and hot in his veins' would not tolerate 'this interference from either prince or priest'. The argument became heated and Angus raised his head and struck the priest with his fist. Whereupon the priest turned round to face the people and prophesied 'Mark my words, it is the hand that struck me today that will part the soul from his body'.

Yet more curses were to be heaped on Angus's head. His sister married a MacDonald from Knoydart who was not doing well and Angus thought he would try and help his brother-in-law. He evicted crofters from an area in Cleadale, gave them the land and built them Cleadale House. The crofters were shipped to America but left 'with great sorrow and lamentation'. They boarded their ship at Rubha Phuirt Bhain in Kildonnan, 'the women weeping and wailing and tearing their hair and calling down a thousand curses on Angus of Laig'. The MacDonald from Knoydart came to Eigg but, when he learned what had been done on his behalf, being a man of 'some compassion and humility', would not stay on the island and returned home. Some time afterwards he fell ill and the doctor gave him a medicine to drink for the terrible pain he got in his bowels. The pain came on one night and his wife got up to fetch the medicine but, feeling for the bottle in the dark, she took the wrong one and poured poisonous dye-stuff into his glass and MacDonald of Knoydart died shortly afterwards. It was said on Eigg that his death was occasioned by the curses called down by the evicted women.

The curse laid on Angus by the priest was also fulfilled. Angus's wife died young and his sister Mary returned to Eigg to look after him and the children, Alan, Donald, Norman, Ronald and Mary. One evening the children went to a gathering on the other side of the island and came home late. When they arrived they found the house empty and, after searching and finding nobody, raised the alarm amongst the neighbours. Angus was found dead about a hundred yards from the house at Na Sitheinean. He had shot himself with his musket which lay by his side. A further search revealed Mary cowering down on the shore in a rock cleft, called *Clach an t-Sionnaich* (Fox's Point), wearing nothing but her night-dress. She had gone out of her mind and, after being brought home, spent the rest of her life locked in one of the rooms at Laig House. Alan inherited Laig, Donald and Norman went to Australia and Ronald joined a shipping company in India as a clerk.

When Ronald went to India he took a portrait of his sister Mary, who was very beautiful, which he kept on his office desk. The man in charge of the office was an Englishman called Bartleman and every time he came into Ronald's room he praised his sister's beauty. When the time came for Bartleman's long leave to England he said to Ronald 'Oh, I'll have to go to Eigg when I am at home in Britain and try to see this beautiful girl, your sister'. This he did and spent a long time on Eigg, eventually persuading Mary to marry him. Bartleman was 'pretty well off in worldly goods' and the family raised no great objection to the match. After the wedding they left Eigg. There was still quite a long spell of Bartleman's leave left and, during this time, news reached Eigg that he was treating Mary very badly. Hearing this, Alan

of Laig decided to try and rescue Mary before the couple set sail for India from Leith. He got a horse from Arisaig and never came out of the saddle, except to change horses, until he reached the pier. He was too late, the ship was heaving anchor and there was nothing for him to do but turn round and go home. Mary died on the voyage and was buried at sea. Alan returned home with the skin rubbed raw off his buttocks and, seeking medical advice, was told that unless he stopped drinking whisky, of which he was a heavy consumer, the injury would never heal. Alan could not give up the drink and the injury ultimately did cause his death.

Alan's drinking sessions mostly took place at Kildonnan. He was a strong man and 'fierce and wild and cross-grained too'. One night when he was coming home 'stone blind drunk' along the cliff face above the Bealach Airigh Leir, where he kept his cattle, he stumbled across, 'a thing' in the dark. This area was believed to be haunted and Alan, thinking he had run into the devil, started to fight, grappling with the creature and trying to get a wrestling grip 'but he might as well have tried to embrace a hogshead'. Next he attempted to push the devil from him and managed to force it over the cliff. When Alan arrived home he described the terrible thing he had met and defeated. The next morning the household got up and when the cowheard went out there was no sign of the bull. They looked everywhere and eventually found it lying dead at the bottom of the gorge. Alan's devil had been his own bull and he had thrown it over the cliff.

Alan married his second cousin Isabel, who came from Inverailort, and as they were both 'well up in years' they had only two children, Angus and Mary. Angus was just twenty when Alan died, leaving 'a load of debt'. 'Poor Alan', describes Hugh MacKinnon, 'he was rather foolish and haughty in his ways and lived in great style beyond his means'. Angus, realising the hopelessness of the situation and that it would be impossible for him to repay the debt from the proceeds of Laig, decided to relinquish the tenancy. In 1853, at the age of 24, he emigrated to America with his mother, sister and cousin, Alan MacAskill, sailing with people evicted from Grulin. Angus got land in Wisconsin and the family settled down. He and his cousin fought in the American Civil War, with the 11th Wisconsin Regiment, but Angus was badly wounded and died a few years later without heirs. Alan MacAskill survived and his descendants live in Los Angeles and one, a lawyer, visited Eigg recently.

KILDONNAN

The largest and richest farm on the island in 1806 was Kildonnan. It amounted to 967.58 acres of which 191.34 was arable, 369.36 pasture and 406.88 moor. The whole settlement consisted of not much more than the farm and mill which also acted as the local change house or sheebin. The tacksman here was Donald MacAskill, the son of the minister Malcolm MacAskill. He had trained as a doctor but preferred to farm and became the Clanranald estate representative on the island. When the crofts were reorganised in 1810 he was put in charge of their allocation and allegations of nepotism were levelled against him when a relative, Niall MacLachain, was given first choice of the plots in Cleadale.

Kildonnan

65

The MacAskills were cousins of the Laig Mac-Donalds and between them the two families controlled the island. Donald probably originally lived in what are now the steadings and barn of Kildonnan farm, as the present house, sited on flat ground by the sea, was not built until 1830. He made his own farm the largest on the island.

Donald was the eldest of three brothers all of whom had a reputation for great strength 'a prized virtue in this society'. This reputation became established while they were quite young when, one Sunday, they went across to Rhum for a church service. At the pier they found some barrels of tar and said to each other, 'He'd be a pretty good man who could lift one of those barrels above his head'. One of them tried, lifting the barrel from the ground to above his head, then letting it down behind his back until it rested between his shoulders, then lifting it again and lowering it gently to the ground. Then the other two did the same 'showing there was no great difference of strength between one and another'. But Donald, when lowering the final barrel slipped and the barrel came down injuring his nose and a stream of blood descended over his chest. When they saw this none of them went to the service that day.

Donald died tragically by drowning within sight of Kildonnan House. He had gone to a cattle fair at Arisaig with his nephew, Alan of Laig, in his boat. Alan returned early in the evening but Donald decided to wait until later and come in another boat along with some cattle, other men and the island tailor. Tacking in the dark, at the entrance to Pol nam Partan bay, the boat overturned. Donald's body was found on the shore the next morning. No one was sure whether he had died while swimming ashore and was washed onto the beach or had collapsed on arrival. The others on the boat managed to reach the shore alive, including the tailor who held onto the tail of a swimming cow and, for ever afterwards, was known as *Taillear a Mhairt*. The cow was later found at Leathad na Bo Runach facing Rhum. It had been sent to Arisaig from Rhum and was trying to get back home.

The two younger brothers left Eigg and had adventurous lives. Alan went to sea and became the captain of a ship which made many voyages in the east. A story is told that once he landed with his crew on an island in the Pacific Ocean and, exploring, they found a cave in which sat a 'great big, wild, ugly old woman' with 'nails on her toes and fingers that were inches long'. She was the queen of the island and reputed to be protecting a hoard of 'riches untold and unaccountable' in her cave. When the Queen saw Alan and his men approaching she made 'as if she was going to spring on them'. The men were terrified and ran away but Alan stood his ground and, drawing his sword, 'split the old woman' and killed her. Riches of every kind were found in the cave which they took away. Alan returned to Eigg later buying an estate called Calgary on Mull. He did not keep if for long, losing it by bragging in a discussion with some people visiting his house, that, if he was offered a certain sum, he would hand over the estate. A man called MacKenzie offered the amount and honour forced Alan to accept.

Ewan, the youngest brother, was the strongest of all. When young he made a running jump at a place below the Manse called *Feith nam Bramanach* covering 33 feet and at one time pegs marked the length of the jump. He also threw a great round stone of white granite, weighing between 25 and 30 pounds, a distance of 30 to 40 feet on the roadway half-way across Eigg on the far side of

Cachaileith na Marbh at *A' Leanag Fhliuch*. Others who tried the same feat failed to throw the stone further than 10 or 12 feet.

Another feat of strength led to Ewan's undoing. As a young boy he went to sea and his ship docked in Liverpool at a time when there was a bully going round the city: a prize fighter who forced the townspeople to pay him money if they could find no one to give him a contest. Ewan asked his skipper if he would give him leave 'to go and have a shot at the bully?' 'Och', said the skipper, 'you can do that but what good is it going to do you to go there. Maybe you'll get yourself killed'. Ewan answered, 'Oh well, be that as it may, I'm going there anyway'.

A fight was arranged, and a meeting place, and 'hundreds and thousands of people gathered to watch the fight'. Ewan and the bully met and within one minute, 'less time than it takes to put it in words', Ewan gave him such a blow his head was split open. The crowd were furious that the fight lasted so short a time and, instead of congratulating 'the sturdy lad who had laid out the bully', they began to chase Ewan. The episode was reported back to Eigg by a lad from Canna who was present and said 'I never saw anything so tragic. There he was running down the streets towards the pier to get on board the ship, and they were after him throwing stones and bottles and anything they could lay their hands on'. Ewan eventually realised he couldn't escape and halted with his back to a wall. The crowd continued to pelt him with 'everything they could lay their hands on but he was just catching it with his hands and keeping them off. In the last resort someone went into the building behind Ewan and, getting a spade, threw it out of the window. The blade pierced the top of his head'. Ewan dragged himself back to his ship, was brought back to Eigg and 'hardly ever put a foot on the ground again as long as he lived', lying in his brother Donald's house at Kildonnan and tended by his mother.

Ewan gave a final demonstration of his strength when, one evening, Donald had some friends to dinner. They were sitting round the table drinking drams from pewter flagons and said to each other, 'He'd be quite a man who could crush a pewter flagon and press the sides of it together'. The mother then went to see Ewan who asked what they were talking about. She told him and he replied, 'You can tell them that one came out of your own body who could do it. You bring me in here the flagon'. She brought him one and 'he crushed it together as you might do a bit of paper. He didn't live long after that and he was still a young man'.

After Donald's death the tack of Kildonnan passed to a Hugh MacDonald from Uist who kept cattle and had eight living-in servants, two agricultural workers and a shepherd. He only stayed a short time and in 1841 a Hugh MacFarlane from Glasgow took the lease. The farm was enlarged to 2,000 acres and planted with potatoes. MacFarlane employed three men, two women and two boys.

Cattle were also kept and grazed during the summer months at Stro on the north end of the island. This was the only shieling on Eigg and the cattle were driven here along a steep cliff path. Hugh Miller describes visiting this lonely place where the ground flattens out under steep hills into boulder-strewn pasture. He says that the shieling was a rude, low-roofed erection of turf and stone with a door in the centre and no windows. Behind the cottage a streamlet poured from the continuous rampart of cliff in a long white thread gathering itself into a lovely little burn which swept past the shieling and expanded into a circular pond where a few 'milch cows slaked their thirst'. A sun-browned island girl of eighteen 'more than merely good-looking' came to the door and invited the visitors inside. Here a turf fire burned at one end round which sat two girls engaged in keeping up the blaze under a large pot. The other end was occupied by a bed of dry straw, spread on the floor from wall to wall and fenced off at the foot by a line of stones. The middle space had utensils and dairy produce, flat wooden vessels of milk, a butter churn, and a tub half-filled with curd, while a few cheeses, soft from the press, lay on the shelf above. Two other inmates were out milking.

Miller came to the conclusion that, lonely though the life of these girls might be, they were better off than those who 'ply their labours in bands among the rich fields of the Lowlands, or for the unwholesome back-room and weary task-work of the city seamstress'. One of the girls did find a companion. At some time during the 19th century a fugitive from the MacLeod country hid in the *Uamh-Chloinn-Diuraidh* cave, at the rocky north point of Stro, and was found by the farmer's daughter who was at the shieling. The fugitive persuaded her to conceal the discovery, even from her father, because 'the inhabitants of Eigg were the natural enemies of every MacLeod. However, from that day his solitude was relieved by occasional meetings with the girl and his hardship alleviated by a share of the produce of the dairy. An attachment sprang up between them but they were scarcely aware of it themselves when the father, Tuathanach nan Coig Peighinn, spotted a strange name on some clothes in the washing. He questioned his daughter, discovered the secret, and was so furious he threatened to shoot the man. The threat had such a distressing

effect on the girl that the farmer relented and instead of shooting the fugitive brought him home, gave him protection and, in the end, the couple married.'

The settlement of Brae lying on the hill above Kildonnan was really part of the farm. There were no crofts here and in 1806 it consisted of eleven houses reduced to seven by 1841. These were lived in by an agricultural labourer, a shepherd, stockman, and 'poor cottager'. During the clearances the cottagers were encouraged to emigrate and shortly after 1851 the last inhabitant left Brae and the Kildonnan farmer constructed a massive sheep fold using the stones from their houses. The elaborate series of stone pens still stand on the hillside but the sheep are now gathered into a fank at Sandavore.

The 'poor cottager' would have been one of several on Eigg. In 1799 there were nineteen protestants and twenty Catholics listed on the kirk session roll. They indiscriminately travelled and received alms throughout the parish and once a year received a donation from the church of 'a little money collected on Sabbaths, and of fines paid by delinquents'.

SANDAVORE, SANDAVEG AND THE GLEBE

Sandavore was originally also a tenanted farm amounting to 259.20 acres divided into 69.79 arable, 23.67 pasture and 165.74 moor. In 1806 it appears to have been a communal farm but by 1818 was taken over by Donald MacAskill and added to Kildonnan. MacAskill also acquired the 383.11 acres of Sandaveg of which 23.45 were arable, 0.45 pasture and 359.21 moor and the 106.06 acres of the adjoining Glebe farm of which 79.19 were arable and 27.87 pasture. Castle Island too was included in the Kildonnan tack. In 1841

The Scurr shrouded in mist taken from above Sandavore

69

the residents of all this land were listed as consisting of agricultural workers, farm servants, stockmen, a shepherd, two teachers, a minister and a merchant.

HOWLAIN

The name comes from the Norse and means 'at or under the hill'. The farm which, in 1806, amounted to 371.35 acres consisting of 67.65 arable, 200.84 pasture and 102.86 moor, lies at the wild and isolated north end of Eigg. The farm house stands white and remote under a dark overhang of hill and was built by Hector MacKinnon who came from Skye. He took the tenancy of Howlain at the end of the 18th century and hand-picked the stones used to build the house. According to Duncan MacKay, 'He was going through the cairns and every stone he could see that would suit he would put a mark on it. Then the labourers came with a horse and sledge and picked up the stone. There were no carts then. And you can see the house is built in rows with square blocks'. It has not been changed. The steading is joined to the house and has an entrance from the hall; upstairs there are two bedrooms and all the rooms are lined with pine-wood. Nearby there are the enclosures MacKinnon built for managing his sheep, the stones taken from uninhabited nearby cottages. Behind the house stand trees planted by MacKinnon.

Howlain was traditionally a cattle farm but, at some point, MacKinnon visited a sheep farmer friend on Skye and decided they were an easier way to make money. However, he had little experience of sheep, mismanaged the operation and went bankrupt. Soon after this experiment MacKinnon relinquished the tenancy and returned to Skye. The farm reverted to the Estate and the house was used by a series of shepherds.

One of these, named Backneau, entered the mythology of Eigg. Duncan Ferguson records that 'In those days the cattle were sent to Glasgow by steamer and it was Backneau's job to accompany the stock. One particular year the tailor who, doing his customary round of the country working so many days in each house, came to Backneau's home for a few days before he left with the cattle. Backneau suspected that the tailor 'was amorous of his wife' and urged him to leave but the tailor refused and insisted on staying to finish his work. During the voyage to Glasgow the crew noticed the shepherd behaving in a 'queer manner'. He began loosing the cattle from their pens and was obviously not in his right mind. Backneau never returned from Glasgow and no one ever knew what happened to him. At home his dogs sat howling for hours every day on the hillside behind the farm. The shepherd's wife told her neighbours she was sure they were howling the name Ardnamurchan and despatched a boat there to look for her husband but the journey was in vain.

Beyond Howlain there was a small farm called Tolain, whose buildings must have been barely discernible amongst the scaley scree and morass of huge rocks that litter the sheer sides of the grey, pinnacled hills that leer over this area of Eigg. The menacing landscape makes the uncanny nature of the stories connected with the farm all the more believable.

The first concerns a changeling child who was left by the fairies in an enclosed field called Creag Cu-Chapull below Bealach Thuilm. The story goes that one day, while working the harvest, one of the women laid her child to sleep in a warm corner of the field. By and by she heard it crying and wanted to go to it but the farmer told her not to until he gave her leave. He knew that the child

Howlain

who was crying was a changeling left by the fairies and that, if it was allowed to cry for long enough, the fairies would take pity on it, take it away and replace the woman's child. This happened but when the mother went to her child she found the fairies, in their resentment, had thrown it on the ground and broken its back.

Another story involves vampires and a shepherd called MacPhee. He was in the hills working the sheep with his three young sons and staying in a hut. One evening the sons came in very tired and went to bed in the sleeping compartment. MacPhee sat up by the fire and, as the night drew on, a small woman entered the door. She came and sat beside the fire and the longer she sat the larger she grew and meanwhile she kept asking MacPhee to go to bed. When he refused she became aggressive and MacPhee's black dog bristled with anger. Dawn came, the cock crew and the woman ran away but was followed by three others who came out of the sleeping compartment. MacPhee's dog pursued the women into the hills and a fight

ensued. The dog was badly mauled and, returning to the hut, dropped dead at MacPhee's feet. When morning came MacPhee went to wake his sons and to his horror found them all dead with tooth marks on their throats. The women had been vampires and had sucked their blood.

A more concrete character was one Ronald MacDonald who came from Glengarry and inhabited Tolain at the same time that MacKinnon lived at Howlain. Black Ronald, as he was known locally, was a bad-tempered man who farmed a few acres but relied for most of his livelihood on smuggling whisky in his boat which was painted white on one side and black on the other. One day he met the revenue cutter and was challenged by the Captain who asked if he had any contraband on board. Ronald answered that his boat was half full of it but the master, Captain Swanson, who was the son of the minister on Eigg, sailed past with the retort that 'if it wasn't you wouldn't be so ready to admit the fact'. Ronald was probably lucky because it was also said that many times

Howlain and the north end of the island

Captain Swanson knew he had contrabrand aboard but, being from the same island, turned a blind eye to the illegal trade. Local tradition records that Black Ronald had two sons, one of whom was 'as bold as his father in the smuggling trade'. Once, when becalmed near Ardnamurchan, he was surprised by the revenue cutter who sent a party to board his vessel. Instead of surrendering, the son fought the party and, getting the upper hand, disarmed them and threw their arms into the sea. He then tumbled them into their dinghies and assured them that 'the government would heal their wounds and nurse them back to health'. For this outrage he was outlawed and, for a long time was hunted unsuccessfully among the Western Isles being hidden by his many friends until he could leave the country. His brother

looked very like him and apparently the police seized him by mistake in Greenock. During the subsequent scuffle he received a wound from which he never recovered.

FIVE PENNIES

This land marched with Howlain and in 1806 amounted to 169.75 acres of which 66.78 was arable and 105.37 pasture. In Norse times a penny land was a unit of taxation. It was the equivalent of about 8 acres and valued as able to support eight cows and two horses. Records show that in 1841 and 1851 there were seven inhabitants at Five Pennies but by 1861 only two houses remained. All the residents are described as being agricultural workers or cottars. They would have been amongst the poorest people on Eigg and, as a

A view of Rhum from Five Pennies

result, easier to move when the land was cleared to make way for sheep. Too poor to afford the passage to America, they probably made their way to livelihoods in the industrial south.

CLEADALE

In 1806 Cleadale was one of the three townships on Eigg; the others being Grulin and Galmisdale. The name in Norse, means 'curved place' and comes from the awe-inspiring amphitheatre of black cliffs that surrounds the green land of the township. Cleadale was divided into three areas: Cleadale, Illtaig and Cuagach totalling 801.60 acres and separated into 194.80 arable, 269.28 pasture and 397.52 moor.

When the crofts were laid out in 1810 the demarcation between Cleadale and Illtaig disappeared. There were four cottars living in Cuagach who, by the end of the 19th century, had either died or gone elsewhere and new crofters were moved in by Lawrence Thompson and given houses. All the arable land in Cleadale was

Lageorna, Donald Campbell's croft in Cleadale

heavily cultivated with oats, potatoes, hay, turnips and beautiful vegetable gardens. 'Today it is very run down and there are few vegetables. People can't be bothered to grow them'.

GALMISDALE

The name is probably derived from the Norse word Galmar-stron meaning 'roaring of the surf'. This can be heard thundering below the rocky cliffs that divides the township of Galmisdale from the sea. In 1789 John MacDonald of Clanranald set aside land here for 'the Towns and Villages presently proposed for Encouragement of the fisheries', but the houses were never built, probably because the sea round Eigg has never been over-endowed with white fish. In 1806 the township is listed as being of 578.82 acres of which 128.84 were arable, 42.92 pasture and 407.06 moor. There were ten houses clustered together inhabited by forty-nine people who, until the 18th century, farmed the land on a communal basis in run-rig fields. When the fields were enclosed the number of inhabited crofts dropped to five. Hugh Miller describes Galmisdale in 1846 as 'consisting of a place mottled with patches of green and studded with dingy cottages, each of which this morning, just a little before the breakfast hour, had its own blue cloudlet of smoke diffused round it'. Later, descending from the Scurr with a companion and feeling weary and hungry, he entered a cottage and asked for something to eat. 'There was a bowl of rich milk brought us, and a splended platter of mashed potatoes, and we dined like princes. I observed for the first time in the interior of this cottage, what I had frequent occasion to remark afterwards, that much of the wood used in buildings in the smaller and outer islands of the Hebrides must have drifted across the Atlantic, borne eastwards

and northwards by the great gulf-stream. Many of the beams and boards, sorely drilled by the *Teredo navalis*, are of American timber, that from time to time has been cast upon the shore – a portion of it apparently from timber-laden vessels unfortunate in their voyage, but a portion also, with root and branch still attached, bearing mark of having been swept to the sea by Transatlantic rivers. Nuts and seeds of tropical plants are occasionally picked up on the beach.'

In the late 19th century the proprietor of Eigg at this time, Lawrence Thompson, decided to base himself in the one large house in Galmisdale. He moved the remaining cottars to Cleadale and with their departure the township effectively ceased to exist as a unit. The old crofts were demolished and the stone used to build the dyke wall that runs up the roadside from the Lodge. All that is left of the old cottages are some platforms which can be seen beside the track leading to Grulin.

Galmisdale House, the name of Thompson's new abode, was originally a croft. It used to be the island inn selling whisky and beer and was also the official court house. In the early years of the 19th century an L-shaped extension was grafted onto the side of the croft and it became a farm in its own right with cattle kept in the fields below the house. The first ferryman, appointed by MacBraynes to meet the steamers, lived at Galmisdale and later it was used to house state employees. An occupant was an old, blind man who lived here with his married son and grandchildren. One day a large ship from the south anchored in the bay below Galmisdale and the son, inquisitive about the boat, rowed out in a dinghy to investigate. Going alongside he began chatting to the Captain who told him he would sell him flour if he had the means to buy it. Returning home the son told his father what the captain had said, commenting that it was a pity they had no money. The old man had a married daughter in Grulin and, later that day, asked his grandson to accompany him on a visit to her. When they reached the boundary between Grulin and Galmisdale, which in those days was a turf dyke, the old man said he could now manage by himself but would rest for a short while first. The grandson, instead of going home as the old man assumed he would, began looking for birds' nests. When the old man thought his grandson was well on his way, he got up and started groping beside the dyke until he came to a certain stone which he pulled out and from behind it removed a jar. On his return home he gave his son enough money to buy some flour from the captain. Shortly afterwards the old man died but without ever divulging from where he obtained the money.

In the 1870's the house was run as a hotel by Donald MacLeod under the name of the Scoor Hotel until Lawrence Thompson decided the Lodge was too enclosed and moved there himself.

Galmisdale House below the Scurr

The shepherd's bothy at Gruilin

GRULIN

The name comes from the Norse word 'grjot' meaning stoney ground. It is an accurate name; great lumps of rock, some the size of houses, lie scattered over the hillside, jettisoned from the enveloping curtain wall of the Scurr ridge. Its primeval blackness glowers over this area of green fields, and heathery hillside, sloping down to cliffs dropping sheer into the sea.

In former times Grulin was divided into two townships, Upper and Lower Grulin. Upper Grulin amounted to 485.25 acres – 59.67 arable, 16.44 pasture, 402.73 moor and 6.41 loch – and the settlement consisted of about eighteen houses. Lower Grulin encompassed 672.82 acres – 54.08 arable, 3.07 pasture, 601.06 moor and 14.01 loch – and had thirteen houses. Together they formed the largest crofting township on Eigg although why this precipitous site, which meets the full force of the westerly gales, should have been chosen is a mystery. It might have been for defensive purposes as the township has been inhabited since ancient times.

The houses are now derelict although their foundations and, in many cases, substantial amounts of wall, still stand. They are joined by a path below which can be seen the old stone-walled animal enclosures. On the hill above there are some curious beehive-shaped huts divided into two. It is not known for what they were used. One theory is that they were used for milking; the cow put in the larger half while her calf was barricaded into the smaller section to keep them separate while the mother was being milked. Others think that they might have been inhabited by monks or hermits as they are similar to the huts at Tolain.

At Grulin the people used to live in small, round-cornered, traditional stone houses. They were built round a circular enclosure with more small animal enclosures beside them. The people kept cattle which had to be herded all day, not just to prevent them pillaging the cottagers' crops but also to protect them from falling over the perpendicular cliffs which, in some places, are 200 feet high. All the ground was dug with lazy beds and their ridges still dissect the entire area. It was a thriving community and many stories are told about the inhabitants.

The most famous was a piper called Donald MacQuarrie who lived here some time after Culloden. He learned his piping from 'that hefty man Ranald MacDonald of Morar, better known as Raonull MacAilein "Og"' who had lands in Arisaig and farmed Sandavore on Eigg. Besides being a famous piper Ranald was also a teacher and composer noted for a difficult piece of music called the *Glas Mheur*. A story is told that when Ranald thought he had taught Donald all he could he sent him to a piper on Skye, called Mac-Crimmon, to see if he could teach him anything more. When Donald played the *Glas Mheur* MacCrimmon sent him away saying, 'Raonull should not have sent you here to mock me'.

Donald, or 'Am Piobaire Mor' as he was also called, was married to a woman from Muck who missed her home and tried to visit her family on every possible occasion. She would signal for her brothers to come and fetch her in their boat by lighting a fire on top of a hill called *Cnoc an Taigh Dhuibh*. The piper became tired of always being left to look after the children and complained to an old man called Domhnall MacCaluim who 'volunteered to cure the wife'. The next time the brothers appeared in their boat Domhnall confronted them and, waving an old sword, he ordered them never to set foot on Eigg again. They never did and the piper had no further trouble from his wife.

Unfortunately, Donald was over fond of the bottle and the drink ultimately caused his death. He used to visit Kildonnan at every opportunity drinking at the mill to all hours of the night. His two sisters were disgusted by his conduct and decided to give him such a fright he would be persuaded to reduce his visits to Kildonnan. On a suitable night they dressed themselves as ghosts, in ankle-length white gowns, and squatted on either side of the road by the burn beyond Galmisdale House, awaiting his return. Soon they heard him coming, tacking from side to side of the road. When he saw his sisters he stopped in his tracks and surveyed the 'ghosts' for a while. As they did not move he imagined he was seeing things but, as he went past, they started to follow him at his own pace. Seeing the apparitions following him he hastened his steps but so did the ghosts. Then, realising he was being pursued, he broke into a run but so did the ghosts. As he was an old man he could not keep up this pace for long and, at last, exhausted, he fell. The sisters, seeing the gravity of the situation, pulled off their 'ghost' gowns and revealed themselves but it was too late. Donald had been given such a fright he never recovered, the sisters had to assist him home and within a short time he died.

His teacher, Ranald MacDonald, hearing of his death, immediately set sail for Eigg to attend the funeral. However, his boat was late and, when the funeral cortege reached the summit above Galmisdale House at Garbh Bhealach, on their way to Kildonnan Church, they paused, waiting for Ranald to arrive. While they waited they built a cairn which, for ever more, has been known as the Carn of Piobaire and still stands by the road. Ranald's boat beached at Pol nam Partan in Kildonnan. He clambered ashore and, swinging his pipes on his shoulder, played them until he met the cortege at the cairn – a distance of three miles uphill. The funeral procession then wound its way to Kildonnan where MacQuarrie is buried.

Another story is associated with Grulin; it is about a beautiful girl called Nighean Bhan Ghrulain or the Fair Maid of Grulin. She was the daughter of a woman called Kate Fraser and was being courted by a local man, Raonull MacIain Bhan, whom 'her parents could have been proud to have as a son-in-law'. However, Nighean was in love with a man on Canna who used to visit her secretly. All the arrangements for her wedding to Raonull had been made but, on a pre-arranged day, her lover sailed from Canna, arriving as she was milking, in the late evening, at the cattle fold which lies about 200 yards from Grulin cottage. The couple repaired with all haste to the chapel where they were married. When Nighean's mother discovered what was happening she hastened after them but she was too late and met them returning from the chapel as man and wife. In a fury the mother took off her boots, aimed one at the groom and bride and the other at the best man and bridesmaid, and cursed all four that none of them would ever have any children. Her curse came true and the best man and bridesmaid never even got married.

One Grulin story illustrates the strength of eagles. A woman who was herding cattle to the west of the township saw what appeared to be a small boat coming directly at her from Rhum. It was travelling very fast and, as it came nearer, she realised the boat was in fact an eagle carrying an object in its talons. The bird was almost exhausted as it reached land but, in spite of this, managed to reach the cliff top where it released its object; a black lamb which, on realising it was free, ran up the hillside. The woman caught the lamb and nursed it back to health and over the years it gave birth to twelve sheep. The eagle had flown a distance of four and a half miles with the lamb, demonstrating 'the great strength and endurance of this noble bird'.

A myth surrounds a girl named Nighean Dhughaill. One day, in the early years of the 19th century, she was herding cattle in the hills when she saw a handsome youth who came and joined her. They sat down and he began to make love to her under the shadow of the Scurr 'but the warm sunshine being stronger than his wooing, he fell asleep with his head in her lap and his hand in her fine black locks'. As the girl gently stroked his fair hair she noticed, to her horror, that it was full of sand and mixed with the leaves of fresh water plants. Then she looked at his feet and saw they were both hoofed and realised that the beautiful youth was in fact a dreaded water kelpie. 'Being of the old Clanranald blood, she neither fainted nor screamed' but, taking a sharp stone, managed to cut her hair free from his hand and lift his head off her lap without him waking. Then she fled for home with the utmost speed but, before she got there, she heard the kelpie's angry voice declaring that he would have her yet. Shortly afterwards the entire population of Grulin were spending a cus-tomary Sunday afternoon chatting together on top of a hillock when the kelpie suddenly appeared in their midst and, seizing Nighean Dhughaill, carried her off before their eyes. The men, with a cry of rage, hastily grabbed some weapons and started in pursuit. They searched everywhere but Nighean was never found, except that 'a piece of her dress and her lungs were seen floating on the surface of a lochan making it only too plain she had met a dreadful end'. Ever since, this lochan has been called by her name.

It is easy to believe that this still, dark, glacial loch holds some evil secret. It lies like a lidless eye in a rugged face, deep in a heathery hollow down the Scurr ridge. Voices echo round its basin and the place has a haunted air as befits its legend. This particular water kelpie story is unusual in Scottish folk-lore because the girl died. Very often once the handsome youth sinks beneath the waters of the loch, he changes into a coarse, old man and the union seldom lasts beyond a year and a day. The girl then escapes and the deserted kelpie can be seen sitting in the evening, nursing their baby, crooning and crying for his wife.

Lochan Nighean Dhughaill

THE SALE OF EIGG

By the end of the 18th century the Clanranalds were in great financial difficulties. The income generated by the reorganisation of their estates and the letting of large farms, amounting to £25,000 a year, was not sufficient for the luxurious, fashionable London society life they now lived. The Clanranald, it was reputed, kept 'seven casks of ruddy wine in his stable, and if a stranger asked what that was for he was told it was the drink for Clanranald's horses. And when the hero went to London he would make his smith shoe his horse with a golden shoe, and only one nail in it; and the horse would cast the shoe in the great street, and the English lords would gather round about it and pick it up and say "Sure the great Clanranald is in London – here is a golden shoe"'. By 1827 the present incumbent, Reginald George Clanranald, an effete man described as 'being more fitted for the soft retirement of an Asiatic harem than the rough country to which he belongs' had spent his entire fortune and was on the verge of bankruptcy. In an effort to remain solvent he began selling land. Both Eigg and Canna went in 1828, to be followed by South Uist in 1837 and Benbecula in 1839.

The island of Eigg was bought by Dr Hugh MacPherson for £15,000. MacPherson already knew the island as his grandfather was the minister at Sleat on Skye and, while staying with him in his youth, he had often visited Eigg and come to 'love and admire it immensely'. When he grew up he became a doctor, joined the Navy as a surgeon and later transferred to the Indian Medical Service, perhaps through the influence of his uncle, Sir John MacPherson, who was secretary to the Nawab of the Carnatic and a member of the Bengal Presidency Council. Sir John acquired great wealth in India and, it is thought, subsidised his nephew's income of £500 a year and, perhaps, the purchase of Eigg. Hugh MacPherson was also a student of ancient civilisations and, when he left India, became professor of Hebrew and Greek at Aberdeen University. One reason for buying Eigg may have been to indulge his interest in archaeology. The island provided fertile ground for his explorations, and his finds from diggings at Kildonnan and on the Scurr are now in the Museum of Antiquities in Edinburgh.

Before taking any decisions on the future of the island MacPherson sent his lawyer, Mr Gordon, to assess the situation. Gordon spent five days on Eigg, starting on Saturday, 24 July, 1828, evaluating the land and listening to the views of both tenants and cottars. He recommended that the boundaries of the farms of Laig, Galmisdale and Kildonnan be revised and new leases given of eight years or nineteen, the latter with a break at the end of eight years, and was strongly impressed with the belief that the 'quality of the grass is better adapted for cattle than sheep pasture' provided turnips were grown for winter food. J. Allan of Laig, who wanted to stock his farm with Blackface sheep, was told his land was better adapted for Cheviots or even South Downs or Leicesters, if he could 'raise some turnips for Hogs'. Gordon noted the names of the cottars and 'most carefully and minutely' inspected each lot, taking account of 'the moss that shows itself in different places' which might be rectified by drainage 'in the hands of a provident tenant of industry and capital', and set a rent of 'about 12/6 per arable Acre'. Everywhere he found the ground 'mopey' and badly in need of drainage and liming but, since the islanders showed little skill in that direction, recommended that a professional drainer with experience of preparing the ground for sheep be employed with the reservation that the ground hardly justified the expense.

The possibilities of the game were also judged. Gordon did not see a single grouse although he was assured that a 'twelve pack' had been viewed recently. To help improve their chances Mac-Pherson had stipulated that all collie dogs be destroyed and Gordon saw 'very few dogs', but the hooded crow, raven and eagles were in evidence and he advised 'encouraging their destruction by means of snares'.

Gordon found the houses, especially the school-house, chapel and Galmisdale, badly in need of repair. He settled a dispute over the mill and made suggestions for new roads but left the island with the view that 'There is apparently not one particle of agricultural skill or science as yet among the Inhabitants'. Taking account of Gordon's recommendations, changes were instigated by Mac-Pherson. He tried to introduce more modern methods of farming but the islanders 'resisted all proposals for the adoption of an improved system of husbandry'. This resistance was perhaps, in part, a rebellion against their new landlord. Abandoned by their traditional chief, they must have felt like orphans placed in the care of a foster parent. Hugh MacPherson appears to have been a stiff and autocratic man and these characteristics may also have fuelled the islanders' antipathy. They certainly had no hesitation in siding with their minister, the Revd. John Swanson, when he swung in favour of the Free Church movement in 1843.

But the seeds of discontent had been sown long before. In 1726, the Established Presbyterian church separated the Small Isles from Sleat in Skye and made them a parish in their own right.

Donald MacQueen was transferred from Uist to be the minister and he lived on Eigg which became the parish headquarters. He was followed in 1757 by the Revd. Malcolm MacAskill who came from the west side of Skye and was known as 'the Strong Minister'. MacAskill believed in the gift of Second Sight and stated in 1763 that he wished 'from the bottom of my heart, that some of my cloth would carry themselves with more decency towards their superiors in most branches of literature, and call to mind that they are only sacred while in the pulpit'.

MacAskill's faith in the supernatural had rather dubious consequences for his wife. She was the daughter of the MacLean, Laird of Coll, and had been forced to marry MacAskill by her family when she was really in love with a MacLeod of Dunvegan. Miserable with MacAskill, she mourned for MacLeod. He became master of a ship based in the north and, when she heard this, she began hoping that one day his ship would sail through the Sound of Eigg and that he would stop for a visit. She began a daily vigil on the edge of the cliffs, waiting for the ship to appear. One day it came under full sail but, to her grief, did not pause and, it is said, the MacLeod never even glanced in the direction of Eigg. Horribly distressed she composed a plaintive song, of which most of the words have been lost. It began with the refrain: 'Though I saw the ship go sailing past, I was looking for the boat being lowered, but there was none and I had no boat or lads to man one so that I could sail out to MacLeod's ship'. The song ended with the wish that 'Maighstir Calum were dead under the boards, And MacLeod and I in the Isle of Man'. It was the last she saw of MacLeod. She stayed with MacAskill long enough to bear him three sons, of whom Donald was tacksman of Kildonnan. She saw them grow up but, at some point, she left MacAskill 'or disappeared or was perhaps murdered'. MacAskill said she had been stolen by the fairies and that he had heard a voice saying that if he got two completely black horses and ploughed a certain knoll in the Kildonnan glebe, his wife would return. But he failed to get the horses and she was never seen again.

Malcolm MacAskill was followed in 1787 by the Revd. Donald MacLean who wrote the classic article on the Small Isles for the *Old Statistical Account of Scotland*. In this he comments on his own role that: 'The King is patron. The living, including manse and glebe, has been, since the augmentation in 1786, equal to about 90l. a year. Of the stipends, 17l. 8s. 9d. has been paid annually out of the teinds of Sleat, since the erection of this parish in a separate charge ... The minister, weather permitting, officiates in Rhum once a month; in Isle Muck once a month; in Canna, once a quarter; and the rest of the time in Eigg. He must attend the meetings of presbytery at Skye, and of synod at Glenelg or Skye, and consequently cannot be above a third of his time at home. He must, at his own expense, keep a boat of a considerable size, and well rigged, always in readiness to transport him to these several islands, which must be a considerable diminution of his income ... The present minister is married, has three sons and two daughters.'

The people of the Small Isles, although predominantly Catholic, were tolerant of both faiths. Thomas Pennant, stopping at Canna during his tour of the Western Isles in 1772, commented, 'I admire the moderation of their congregations who attend the preaching of either [priest] indifferently as they happen to arrive ... The Scotch are economists in religion'. Dr Johnson described Eigg as 'a Popish island' in his *Tour of the Hebrides*,

1775. He and Boswell planned a visit to Eigg but storms prevented their landing. They had to content themselves with looking at the island from the sea, on their voyage to Coll, and hearing the story of the cave massacre from their host, Donald MacLean of Coll, Hugh Miller said that 'the parish minister lived on the best possible terms with the Popery of the Island' and that 'all was harmony between the churches'.

This happy state of affairs was not to continue. The Established church continued to make inroads into the Western Isles. Their evangelising did not affect the Clanranalds who kept their Catholicism, but thereby forfeited the right, granted to landlords in 1777, to choose their own ministers, and the incumbent for the Small Isles was accordingly appointed by the Crown. An elegant church and manse were built by the Established church in 1793 for the use of the minister on Eigg.

Neil MacLean was appointed by the Crown in February 1811. He exemplified the Establishment, being the son of the factor on Rhum and Muck and married to the sister of Dr MacLean, tenant of Rhum. Besides being Small Isles minister he was also a substantial farmer, cultivating the Glebe, Sandavore and Castle Island, and rose to become Deputy Lieutenant of Inverness-shire. His position of minister and his close relationship with Dr MacLean of Rhum were to assist his downfall. The ministers of the Established church frequently condoned the worst excesses of the Clearances and Neil MacLean had not raised much protest when his father-in-law evicted the people of Rhum, in a particularly brutal and summary fashion, to make way for sheep.

When, in 1834, it was revealed that the minister had been leading a double life, the full force of the people's law fell on his head. MacLean was charged with multiple adultery, attempted rape, indecent exposure, assault, giving an oath 'regarding some woman' before his Catholic colleague, drunkenness on foot and horseback, and neglect of his duty. The lurid evidence included the accusation that he had been found in bed with two women. On the 9th September his case was heard by the Skye Presbytery, acting as prosecutor, judge and jury, at the Inn of Eigg at Galmisdale, until an 'unseemly racket from the nearby beer tent' made them move to the school. The case dragged on and was moved to the General Assembly in Edinburgh. MacLean's drinking was very public. According to Hugh Miller he was 'by far the best customer' of the public house on Eigg, 'a ruinous two-gabled house beside the boat harbour'. Here 'he was in the practice of sitting in one of its dingy little rooms, day after day, imbibing whisky and peat-reek; and his favourite boon companion on these occasions was a Roman Catholic tenant who lived on the opposite side of the island, and who, when drinking with the minister, used regularly to fasten his horse beside the door, till at length all the parish came to know that when the horse was standing outside, the minister was drinking within.'

MacLean added insult to injury when, in 1838, he wandered in drunk to the General Assembly to hear one of his numerous appeals. The company were appalled and removed him from office. MacLean died the following year, destroyed by the court case and his heavy drinking. He may have been guilty of some of the charges but he was also the victim of much resentment arising from the Clearances.

Neil MacLean was succeeded by John Swanson who was of quite a different mould. A former grocer and schoolmaster, he was virulently anti-Catholic and had even published a Gaelic pamphlet against Popery. His puritan outlook probably endeared him to MacPherson, embittered by the scandals caused by MacLean's behaviour. However, Swanson's piety was to be the cause of another religious upheaval on Eigg. The right of the laird to choose the minister began to be questioned by congregations and members of the Kirk Sessions – lay elders who maintained the theocratic idea laid down by the Reformation. In 1843, when 474 members of the clergy seceded to form the Free church, many supported this religious schism which became known as 'the Disruption'. The landlords, disgruntled by the long dispute and its result, refused sites to the Free church on which to build new churches, and the people gathered where they could to hold services.

The Revd. John Swanson was a leading supporter of the Free church movement and of the Gaelic Schools Society. These schools were founded to augment those run by the SPCK who had now dropped their anti-Gaelic policy. The new society was non-sectarian and non-political and concerned to teach children 'to read in their native language'. The 'want of schools' was another complaint of the *Statistical Account* in

1798. It says that 'the school created by the SPCK was removed in 1792 and the parochial school, established in 1793, was unsatisfactory because it was 'fixed on Eigg, and the only one in the parish. From this school, children in the other islands, especially the poorer sort, can derive no benefit. Ignorance must be the consequence, and they may not only be an early prey to seducers, but worse qualified to act their part as useful members of society. To obviate this grievance, a school, if practicable, should be established in each island.' In 1812 the Gaelic School Society set up peripatetic schools that stayed in one place between six and eighteen months and were enthusiastically attended on the Small Isles. The Inverness Society sent the Small Isles 92 Gaelic Bibles and 105 New Testaments in about 1819 which made, according to Father Anthony MacDonald, 'a wonderful change . . . formerly [the people] devoted the Sabbath entirely to idle conversation or frivolous amusements . . . now they regularly . . . read the Scriptures . . . in many instances the parents are instructed by the children'. A school was opened where besides children 'many adults, from forty to fifty years of age were induced to go to school'. In 1828 the proprietor, Dr MacPherson, ordered windows and 150 slates costing 10/6 for the repair of this school house and later a wing was added 'to the tenement, having at present but one apartment for Kitchen, Parlour, and Hall,' and the schoolmaster with 'a breeding wife and ten children'. Things had deteriorated by 1836 as Father Donald MacKay wrote that 'The present schoolmaster is not noted for the attention of his scholars, or diligence in the discharge of his duties. He seldom has more than twenty or thirty scholars and often he has none, the parents withholding them from school, knowing that they make no progress in their education under him'. MacKay

also complained that the Gaelic schoolmaster was hostile to him and his pupils and had tried to prejudice the proprietor, MacPherson, against him. The Gaelic Schools Society collapsed with the Disruption but Swanson kept the movement alive on Eigg. In 1830 he had a school house built from his own money, feeling that if English were taught the young people would go to the cities and never return. In 1843 a Report of the Gaelic Schools Society referred to 'the excellent minister of the parish, the Revd. Mr Swanson' and the fact that he, with the help of the schoolmaster, Donald MacKinnon, had rescued the population which was still half Catholic 'and the Protestants . . . almost Papist at heart'.

Swanson's support of the Free Church movement met opposition from MacPherson who was a staunch advocate of the Established church and refused a site for either church or manse on Eigg. The people petitioned the proprietor but got no reply. After months the factor came to Eigg and told the islanders 'that it was not likely the Doctor would permit a *third* place of worship on the island; the Roman Catholics had one, and the Establishment had a kind of one, and there was to be more'. In spite of the fact that the Established church was in such need of repair 'the Congregation were put to their shifts to keep themselves dry' during a rainstorm, a second petition was also refused, and by this time Swanson, reduced to 'heroic poverty', based his family on Isle Oronsay, Skye, and made his small, 30 foot yacht, the *Betsy*, his religious base. Throughout the summer months he cruised the Western Seas preaching to the islanders in 'black houses and on the beaches'. Douglas Simpson says in his *Portrait of Skye and the Outer Hebrides* that 'Whatever opinion may be held about the rights and wrongs of the Disruption, nothing but admiration can be

felt for such self-sacrificing devotion, and for the staunch loyalty of the faithful who clung to their dispossessed pastor'.

In June 1844 Swanson invited Hugh Miller, a lifelong friend, ardent geologist and author and editor of the *Witness* (one of the few papers to champion the cause of the Free church) to accompany him and pursue his geological studies on board the *Betsy* for a three-week cruise. Miller accepted and his account of the voyage, *The Cruise of the Betsy*, is not only one of the most brilliant books on early geological literature but also gives a graphic account of life on Eigg and of Swanson's evangelising. Afloat on the Free church yacht they were not very secure, when nights were dark and winds loud, but at least were beyond reach of 'man's intolerance, and not beyond the protecting care of the Almighty'. The cabin of the boat was about the size of a common bed and only high enough for a man of 'five feet eleven to stand erect in his nightcap'. A large table, lashed to the floor and covered with a writing desk, occupied the narrow middle space, there were two seats in front of the stove, a barred skylight from which hung a 'lanthorn-looking lamp' giving a dim light. The peculiar furniture 'gave evidence of the mixed nature of my friend's employment. A well-thumbed chart of the Western Isles lay across an equally well-thumbed volume of Henry's *Commentary*. There was a polyglot and a spy-glass in one corner, and a copy of Calvin's *Institutes*, with the latest edition of *The Coaster's Sailing Directions* in another; while in an adjoining state-room, nearly large enough to accommodate an arm-chair . . . a printing press and his case of types, canopied overhead by the blue ancient of the vessel, bearing in stately six-inch letters of white bunting, the legend FREE CHURCH YACHT'.

In July they arrived at Eigg, passing 'the Isle of Muck with its one low hill'; and the 'colossal Scurr' which rose 'between us and the sky as if it were a piece of Babylonian Wall'. After casting anchor, getting warm and comfortable over the stove and some tea, they went to bed. In the morning they had a 'rich tea . . . The minister was among his people and our first evidence of the fact came in the agreeable form of three bottles of fresh cream from the shore. Then followed an ample baking of nice oaten cakes. The material out of which the cakes were manufactured had been sent from the minister's own store aboard – for oatmeal in Eigg is rather a scarce commodity in the middle of July; but they had borrowed a crispness and flavour from the island, that the meal, left to its own resources, could scarcely have communicated; and the golden-coloured cylinder of fresh butter which accompanied them was all the island's own. There was an ample supply of eggs too, as one not quite a conjuror might have expected from a country bearing such a name – eggs with the milk in them; and, with cream, butter, oaten cakes, eggs and tea, all of the best, and with the sharp-set sea-air appetites to boot, we fared sumptuously'.

They were not made welcome by the proprietor. His hostility was shown when Miller, who used his time ashore to thoroughly investigate the geology of Eigg, climbed the Scurr with Swanson. They were warned off by a messenger from 'a Roman Catholic tacksman in the neighbourhood' who stated that 'the Scurr of Eigg was the property of Dr MacPherson of Aberdeen, not ours, and that the Doctor would be very angry at any men who meddled with it'. A message, Swanson asserted, that 'would scarce have been sent us when I was minister of the Establishment here; but it seems allowable in the case of a poor

Dissenter and is no bad specimen of the thousand little ways in which the Roman Catholic population of the island try to annoy me, now they see my back to the wall'.

Finally the Sabbath arrived, 'the morning rose like a hypochondriac wrapped up in his nightclothes – gray in fog, and sad with rain'. Miller and Swanson 'set out for church a little after eleven'. The service took place in the 'low dingy cottage of turf and stone' which had been built by Swanson for his Gaelic school. They found the 'congregation already gathered and that the bad morning had failed to lessen their numbers'. Miller noted that the people of Eigg 'are an active, middle-sized race with well-developed heads, acute intellects and singularly warm feelings'.

The rude turf building was 'full from end to end, and all a-steam with a particularly wet congregation, some of whom, neither very robust nor young, had travelled in the soaking drizzle from the farther extremities of the island. And, judging from the serious attention with which they listened to the discourse, they must have deemed it full value for all it cost them. I have never seen a congregation more deeply impressed, or that seemed to follow the preacher more intelligently; and I was quite sure, though ignorant of the language in which my friend addressed them, that he preached them neither heresy nor nonsense'.

Dr MacPherson later relented and subsequent Free church ministers used a cottage opposite the present shop as a church. The Free church did not retain its hold over the people of Eigg; they eventually rejected this religion with its rigorous adherence to a spartan way of life, its denial of music and dancing, and indeed, most of the other pleasures of life. By the 1930s their ministers had left the Small Isles but not before they had caused the death of much folk-lore and Gaelic culture – a fact of which they were proud. Swanson is quoted as saying that 'It is a not uninteresting fact that my poor people, since they have become more earnest about their religion, think very little about ghosts and spectres: their faith in the realities of the unseen world seems to have banished from their minds much of their old belief in its phantoms.'

The influence of the Free church is further seen in the story of the MacKays' violin. The MacKay family came to Eigg from Muck in 1810 at the invitation of Angus MacDonald of Laig. He had heard Donald MacKay playing the violin and, being a keen musician, offered him a good house and croft if he would come and live on Eigg. MacKay arrived but when he saw the house in Cleadale he decided it was too big, especially since he was a weaver by trade and preferred this to farming. At the time, the parish priest, Father Anthony MacDonald, was living in a house that was too small at Sandavore. They agreed to swop houses and Cleadale House, or rather its second version, remained the priest's house. The violin Mackay played was given to him by MacLean of Coll who had bought it from a sailor travelling to Italy. What none of them knew was that the violin was in fact a Stradivarius. MacKay's son Neil was also a good violinist but, as none of his family were particularly interested and as he had been convinced by a Free church missionary from Lewis that he would go to Hell if he continued to play music, he willingly sold it to a dancing master called MacDougall. He was on the island giving lessons and paid 11/- for the violin. When the dancing master opened the violin and saw the name of Stradivarius he exclaimed 'My fortune is made'. He sold the instrument to a man who is said to have sold it again to an Edinburgh museum.

The middle years of the 19th century were ones of hardship for most of the people of Eigg due to the continuing problem of over-population. In 1831 the schoolmaster commented that 'There is an abundant population on the island at present. Consequently, when there is a failure of their small crops, which is too often the case, especially of late years, the poor are doomed to suffer much privation and destitution. They would gladly follow their friends to Her Majesty's colonies in North America where a great many of the inhabitants of the Small Isles have emigrated several years ago, but in their present circumstances I do not think that the most of them are able to even pay their passage across the Atlantic . . . and there has been no emigration from the island in the previous six years'. The poverty that resulted from this situation was noted by Queen Victoria when she sailed within sight of Eigg in 1847 and wrote in her diary that 'At one o'clock we were in sight of the Isles of Rum, Eigg and Muck'. She mistakenly believed that they were all owned by Lord Salisbury, saying that these 'rather large islands which Lord Salisbury bought a few years ago . . . have, unhappily, been terrible sufferers during the last winter from famine'.

Statute labour schemes helped some of the poverty, building both the road and Clanranald's pier. In 1798 the road on Eigg was 'almost in a state of nature' and there was 'not a bridge in the whole parish' in spite of the fact that 'several of our waters become often dangerous, and even impassible, by heavy falls of rain and melting snow'. MacPherson's lawyer made recommendations for extending the road and connecting various settlements. In 1836 one was built linking the main places on Eigg: the pier, Kildonnan, Cleadale and Grulin. All the work was done by the islanders. In most cases it was more a question of giving the existing cart-track a hard bottoming of stones, but they had no machinery and all the work was done with a pick and shovel.

Much of the statute labour performed in the different islands was 'directed towards the building of piers, for the accommodation of fishing boats and vessels of an inferior size'. They were ill-conceived and complaints were raised that they were not 'conducted on a plan of the most liberal and useful, nor has any of them hitherto been carried to perfection'. Certainly the one on Eigg, known as Clanranald's Pier, situated across the bay from the present edifice, aptly sums up

Clanranald Harbour

91

the remark made by Stanford that 'A Highland quay is a quarter of a mile from the sea at low tide and completely submerged at high tide'. The statute labour was probably used to improve an existing structure because the *Statistical Account* mentions a pier 'built by the inhabitants for the security of fishing boats and small vessels' but continues that 'it has been neglected for some time, and become in a manner ruinous'. The new pier was placed on the old pitchstone dyke and built in a horse-shoe shape; a crude structure of enormous black, basalt stone now falling into disrepair. It was here that Hugh Miller landed in 1844 and he describes 'a deserted boat-harbour formed of loosely piled stone, at the upper extremity of a sandy bay'. The weather was not good and he continues in a bleak fashion:

'The entire scene suggested the idea of a land with which man had done for ever; the vapour-enveloped rocks – the waste of ebb-uncovered sand – the deserted harbour – the ruinous houses – the melancholy rain-fretted tides eddying along the strip of brown tangle in the foreground – and, dim over all, the thick slant lines of the beating shower! I know not that of themselves they would have furnished materials enough for a finished picture in the style of Hogarth's "End of all Things".'

One advantage that Eigg had over the mainland was that it was not afflicted by the potato blight which caused such misery and starvation in other places. MacFarlane, the farmer who took the tack of Kildonnan around 1841, exploited this to his full advantage. He imported tram horses from Glasgow, attached them to ploughs, and with the

Ancient stone circles above Gruilin

help of his employees and every other available hand on the island, dug all the land from Kildonnan to Cuagach. This was planted with potatoes and every week loads left by puffer to feed the starving on the mainland from a pier MacFarlane built by Kildonnan farm.

Another farmer who exploited Eigg at this time was Stephen Stewart who came from Kirkcudbrightshire. After the MacDonalds left Laig in 1853 he took the tack and offered Dr MacPherson a higher rent if the townships of Upper and Lower Grulin were also included as he wanted the land for sheep grazing. Dr MacPherson agreed and the fifteen resident crofters were told to leave. All but two families were shipped to Nova Scotia. Their houses were allowed to crumble except for one bothy which was lived in by the shepherd, Hector MacQuarrie, and exists today. The other family who remained were the MacCormicks. They were saved by Mor MacCormick's father-in-law, Neil MacQuarrie, who was reluctant to see his daughter go to America. He had another croft in Cleadale besides the one he was working himself. Here, Findlay and his wife Mor moved with their one horse and stock of five cows that they had kept on a pennyland at Grulin. However, the cows missed their old home and one morning, exactly a year later, when Findlay let them out they made off down the road heading for their old home. Findlay pursued them but they travelled too fast for him and never halted until they reached Grulin. He rounded them up and drove them back to Cleadale and they never strayed again. Neither did Findlay MacCormick and his descendants, of whom one, Angus MacKinnon, still inhabits the same croft.

Hugh MacKinnon recorded that 'Our proprietor was like plenty of other proprietors in the Highlands at the time, and the evictions did not trouble his conscience very greatly. It was just a case of telling the poor crofters who were in Grulin that they would have to clear out, and there was nothing else for it; they just had to turn out at Whitsun in the year 1853 and take themselves off to America'.

The first year, owing to the excellent condition of the land left by the evicted crofters, the grass was so sweet all the ewes had twins. Stephen Stewart was one of the new breed of innovative border sheep farmers. Besides putting sheep on the fertile, sloping fields of Grulin he also made moves to improve the rest of his land. Thirty acres of marshland round Laig were drained. The drainage of this land was recommended by Mac-

Pherson's lawyer in 1828 and, in the 1840s, Angus MacDonald was asked if he would consider a government-sponsored drainage scheme to provide employment. Angus was already thinking of emigrating and refused, but Stewart reintroduced the idea and to oversee the operation brought in two expert drainers from the Borders, George and David Kirk. All the work was done by hand as there were no mechanical implements in those days. Once the drains were finished the Kirk brothers left, but one, David, returned and became Stewart's shepherd. After a few years he again left, but his job was taken by his son Donald, and his descendants now live at Laig.

Stephen Stewart's management of his horses caused comment. The islanders fed their horses by grazing them at the end-rigs while they were working in the fields, but Stewart stabled his, feeding them on straw and oats, to make them fitter for work. They were only let out when the spring work was finished, which sometimes lasted until the end of June, and in August, when the haymaking began, they were again stabled. During wet weather, if the horses were unable to work, they were exercised by being ridden round the island and back by Laig beach where they were walked through the sea. Stewart believed that salt water was an antidote for grease, the infection that affects the legs of heavy work horses.

In 1871 Stewart relinquished the tack of Laig. He perhaps foresaw the collapse of the wool market and the agricultural depression that affected the whole of Britain in the 1880s. Roderick MacRae from Ross-shire then took the tack, but not for long, and after him came a Peter Cameron from Ayrshire who farmed Ayrshire cows. He used their milk for making butter and cheese, much of which was sold on the mainland.

Hugh MacPherson died in 1854 after a long illness. He had not been seen on the island since 1841 and his farms were managed by a factor.

Eigg desperately needed some overall direction at this time. The people were very poor, afflicted by the general depression occasioned by the disastrous failure of the potato crop on the mainland. They appealed for help when 'Two sacks of meal were left and starvation was imminent' but met an unsympathetic ear in MacPherson's factor and lawyer, both of whom lived on the east coast. They answered that as far as they could see all 'was satisfactory . . . there was a supply of food on Eigg . . . the landlord's liability was limited and the people idle and apathetic'. MacPherson's daughter, Christina, defended her father, writing that 'Papa has, I am sorry to say, suffered at the utmost possible extent receiving no rent, and feeding many hundreds of people in Eigg a position you must feel . . . to be by no means a convenient one'.

MacPherson left Eigg to his numerous children. The most notable was Norman, who was Professor of Scots Law at Glasgow University. An academic, he came to Eigg and 'talked a great deal but did nothing'. Another daughter, Isabella, took up residence on Eigg. She eulogised that the high population was due to the fact that 'no one will move, they all adore the place' and became the island's 'uncrowned queen'. For fifty years she lived on the island, planted many of the trees round the lodge and stocked the lochs with trout.

By the 1870s the depression had passed and Eigg was relatively prosperous. Potatoes, sheep and cattle were making money but when, in the 1880s, farm prices collapsed as a result of cheap imports from the New World, they shared in the fall. In 1886 the Crofters Holding Act came to the aid of the islanders whose inability to 'express their grievances in English, the language of parliamentary democracy, had all too frequently kept their voice unheard'. The Crofters Holding Act, which was described as 'the Magna Carta of the Hebrides', heralded not so much a new era but actually perpetuated small, uneconomic holdings and succeeded in insulating crofting from the mainstream of agriculture. Crofting land was both unproductive and unprofitable, the islands desperately needed some new development but they were given stagnation.

In 1883 the Royal Commission, under Lord Napier, visited most of the crofting areas of the Highlands and Islands but not, it appears, Eigg. Their report states that there are twenty-eight crofters on the island each making a living on between 3–5 acres, plus their share of common grazing, on which they keep three cows and their progeny. The Act gave the islanders increased rights and land. Crofts were allocated of various sizes, giving grazing for from one to four cows, but by annexing vacant crofts some people kept as many as ten to twelve cows. Fifty acres of common grazing was allowed for their horses on Ben Buidhe. The allocation of land was done on paper from the mainland with little knowledge of the actual lie of the land. In reality the arable land was smaller than estimated by the Commission and the crofts were not able to grow enough winter feeding for the croft to be stocked according to the 'souming' or proportion of animals allowed on the common grazing. An added disadvantage was that the common grazing on Ben Buidhe was too high to be easily reached by the crofters.

Ruined house at Cleadale

WAY OF LIFE

Until the beginning of this century life on Eigg followed a deeply entrenched pattern perpetuated by families associated since ancient times with the Western Isles. In the annals of Eigg certain surnames predominate: MacDonald, MacLellan, MacLeod, MacLean, MacKinnon, MacQuarrie, Kirk, Robertson, Campbell and MacKay. They marry and intermarry and produce large numbers of children, often five or six and sometimes ten and twelve. The children are called after their parents or grandparents, the same names recurring in different combinations as the families become interwoven, creating confusion to the outsider. In the 19th century the children occasionally went to school but always helped on the croft. When they grew up those who could stayed on Eigg farmed and practised other trades such as tailor, blacksmith and fisherman. Those who found no work, left. People with money for the fare went to America, Canada and Australia. Many of the rest joined professions connected with the sea whose habits they knew so well; the Navy or the shipyards of Glasgow. The girls worked as servants in the larger houses on Eigg or became nurses in Glasgow hospitals. Some, drawn by their roots, eventually returned to Eigg.

Their histories were passed on in the oral tradition. In this century a few descendants wrote or told what they remembered of life lived on the island. Most notable are Kenneth MacLeod's, the son of the schoolmaster on Eigg who became a conscious collector of island traditions at a young age and later collaborated with the Celtic Revivalist, Marjorie Kennedy-Fraser, to produce the four volume book, *Songs of the Hebrides*. Hugh MacKinnon, who died in 1972, was the last on Eigg with the true oral tradition and his recollections were recorded by the School of Scottish Studies. Duncan Ferguson, shepherd to the Runcimans, proprietors of Eigg from 1925 to 1966, wrote his own account and today Duncan MacKay and Angus MacKinnon hold a wealth of stories in their memories.

Colin Carr, farm manager, and Neill MacDonald, shepherd on Eigg

Angus MacKinnon

FARMING

The farming year began in spring when the fields were manured with seaweed gathered from the shore and lime taken from a seam on the north-west side of the island. It was burnt in lime-kilns, several of which still exist in Cleadale. The land was then ploughed. By the 19th century the old foot-plough or 'cas-chrom' had been largely re-placed by primitive horse-drawn wooden ploughs which caused an outsider to remark that, in the Highlands, 'everything is done by rude strength and perseverance'. Later, iron ploughs arrived and then, in 1947, the first tractor which 'revolu-tionised the whole system of cultivation and harvesting'.

After ploughing came seed time. The main crops grown were potatoes, turnips, hay and oats. Quantities of potatoes were planted of several varieties, Mid-Lothian, Edzell Blue, Kerr's Pink, Golden Wonder, Langworthy, Arran Coracle and Arran Banner, nine cwt being the average return from a cwt of seed. Only the estate grew turnips of any scale, using them for winter feed for the animals. The crofters just had enough to make into soup and other domestic dishes. Hay was collected for winter feed. Duncan Ferguson des-cribes how 'in the old days . . . It was a fine sight to see six stalwarts cutting hay with the scythes and all swinging in time, taking an average of 8 feet width and about a foot to 15 inches on each swipe. Sometimes these men would be days on end cutting with the scythe and they loved it. Starting at 7 a.m. until 6 p.m. and sometimes up to 9 or 10 p.m. during the busy time'. After cutting, the grass was allowed to dry in swathes unless rain threatened when it was forked into little 'coils' or hay cocks. The hay was spread out and gathered many times before it was completely dry.

Oats were the main crop. The average return on seed sown was often pitifully low; one ear for every ten to twelve seeds and, in good years, five or three. This was hardly surprising in view of the lateness of the harvest and liability to storm damage. The corn was cut by the men with sickles and sheaved and stacked by the women. They sang as they worked. A traveller, E. Burt, wrote that 'they all keep time together, by several barbarous Tone of the Voice; and stoop and rise together as regularly as a Rank of Soldiers when they ground their Arms'. John Leyden likened their singing to the 'screaming of gulls' but Kenneth MacLeod takes a more romantic view of the scene. 'In the days when they grew barley and oats on the ridges and furrows the Gruagach, a woman of the other-world, was standing on Laig Brae watching along with a mystic of the isle, the reaping of the fields of Cleadale. The waving croon rose and fell, like the waves of Laig Bay, the lilt of reaping song: Heiteagan airin hu ho-i-ro. "O Ian Oag" said the woman "the making of the bread, is it not the gladsome thing." The mystic answered, 'And so it should be yet the reaping-song has never been one of pure joy. To the singing goes the life of a year, the summer that is gone and winter that is coming, the ones who have sown but are not here to reap; the ones who will sow when the reapers here have forgotten; the Good Being who makes the sun shine and the corn ripen, who opens the ear to the singing sands of Morar and the eye to the phantom kingliness of the Coolins of Rum and the Coolins of Skye. To the harvest field we go for life as it ought to be. The sickle is fate, the hand that holds it ours and for once we will be the conquerer. Cut we down a sorrow here and a pain there, bind them and make them our slaves. Sure then, this is the glad day and the beautiful world, and the brave life – what we shall afterwards dream of in the long winter night.'

The islands were seldom self-sufficient in grain and frequently had to import supplies especially after severe winters when a greater part of the crop was fed to the cattle. These were the islanders' most important animals. In the Highlands the land and climate has always been more suitable for raising livestock and from remote times they have depended on them to provide the money to supplement their supplies of corn, buy necessary items such as iron and pay the rent. From Norse times all land was valued for tax by the number of cattle it could carry. They sub-divided land into the components of an ounce of silver; merklands, pennylands and farthinglands. On Eigg opinions are divided as to what constituted a pennyland. Some said it was a croft capable of carrying four cows, their followers and a horse, while others two cows and a horse. In roadless days cattle could transport themselves to market and if their route was disrupted by war the people suffered great hardship.

On Eigg, every May, drovers would arrive from Arisaig and other parts of the mainland to buy cattle. In the old days the drovers would call at each croft and argue a price but latterly they held a sale at Sandavore, in the steading by the Glebe roundabout, 'and they were buying all the stock and you were clear of it'. These 'horned, wild, rough cattle of all possible colours' were then roped by the horns, loaded into open boats and sailed across to the mainland where they were unloaded by being thrown overboard and left to swim ashore. Their destination was the tryst at Crieff and markets in the Midlands. In later years they were taken out to a ferry and hoisted aboard in a sling. Loading the cattle was a laborious business and Duncan MacKay remembers 'You were black and blue by the time you had finished'. Now they are driven aboard a landing craft 'and it is so much easier'. They are sold at the market in Fort William or Oban.

Cattle were seldom eaten on Eigg. Each crofter kept his own bull and a permanent stock of cows used for breeding and milking which was made into butter, cheese, crowdie, cream and curds. Surplus milk was fed to the calves from pails. Milking took place from May to the end of summer and was considered women's work. 'There weren't many of the men that would milk,' remembers Duncan MacKay. The girls sang as they stripped the milk from the cows, performing the task in the open. These two plaintive airs were collected on Eigg by Kenneth MacLeod.

O HEARTLING OF MY HEART

A moaning thou, My own dear one,
A moaning thou, Heartling Heart,
A moaning thou, My own dear one,
Sad moaning thou, Heartling Heart,
'Mong yon cattle on the meadow,
See'st yon calfling by its mother led,
He ho-li-kan, Ho My-er, Hey ho-li-kan,
My-er-oo! See'st yon bramble bush a near her,
Bending laden with its berries red,
Hey ho-li-kan, Ho my-er, Hey ho-li-kan,
My-er oo. One cause of my sorrow
Thou, my dear one, My Heartling Heart,
Links thee to me, Keening thou thy calf,
Thy dear one, keening I my son 'neath the sea.
Hey-ho-li-kan, Ho-my-er,
Sad keening I my son neath the sea.

THE ISLE OF ST. DONNAN

Milking the cattle on the face o' Corravine,
Dew o' the skies on the face o' Corravine,
Milking cattle on the face o' Corravine,
Youth for age on the face o' Corravine.

Yonder see I the Isle o' the Deer,
Yonder see I the Scurr to the sky,
Yonder see I the Isle o' the Deer,
The rugged bens o' my love, to the sky.

Milking cattle on the face o' Corravine,
Dew o' the skies on the face o' Corravine,
Milking cattle on the face o' Corravine,
Youth for age on the face o' Corravine.

Early puts the sun greeting on Stro-a,
Early chant the birds the beauty o' Donnan,
Early puts the sun greeting on Stro-a,
Early grows the grass on the Shieling o' Donnan.

The warm eye o' Christ on the tomb o' Donnan,
The stars so high on the tomb o' Donnan,
The warm eye o' Christ on the tomb o' Donnan,
No ill, no ill on the tomb o' Donnan.

Milking cattle on the face o' Corravine,
Dew o' the skies on the face o' Corravine,
Milking cattle on the face o' Corravine,
Youth is age on the face o' Corravine.

Except for those at Kildonnan the cattle on Eigg were not taken to upland shielings for the summer. They were carefully watched and herded during the day to prevent them breaking into arable ground and housed throughout the year at night. In winter they were housed during the day as well and fed hay and corn. In early days they shared their owner's residence, living in stalls at one end of the house. These were generally placed on the windward side so that the cows generated extra heat. Later, when the crofters built new houses, the old residence became the byre. The hens also lived in the house, roosting in the rafters at night. Cocks were sacred and a power against the evil of darkness. In Gaelic their name, *Fear bheannachaidh na Maidne*, means 'he who blesses the morning' and few would walk abroad until after the cock had crowed. The people ate huge quantities of eggs, their flesh made a valuable addition to their sparse, winter diet and on South Uist they formed part of their rent.

The crofters kept few sheep. On Eigg only the large farms allowed both big numbers of sheep and for them to roam free. It is still the law that crofters' sheep have to be either confined or tethered. They never had more than enough to provide wool for spinning. Six or seven was the general number and, after the 18th century, these were of the Blackface or Cheviot breed; the latter producing softer, finer wool more suitable for making into clothes and blankets. With the influx of the new lowland breeds came the Border collie dog; yellow-eyed, bright, intelligent and canny.

Every crofter had a horse until the early years of this century. They ran loose on the common grazing above Ben Buidhe until wanted for farm work when they were caught, led down the steep, zig-zag cliff path and kept tethered at the end of the out-rig. The *Statistical Account* of 1798 mentions that the horses were 'hardy and high-mettled, though of small size'. The islands tended to develop their own variations and there are still distinct breeds on Barra, Rhum and Eriskay. On Eigg, the horses were basically of Highland stock but there were crosses and larger ones which came from Uist. They were used for ploughing, carting and bringing home the peats. Duncan MacKay says there were seventeen horses in his young days. 'They were tough, and they could pull.'

As well as working the croft all the men did some fishing. They caught skate, cod and conger eels on long lines. Most of these fish were preserved to supplement the winter diet by being laid out on walls in the sun to dry and 'like that they would last for years'. Lobster, crab and prawns were caught in baited creels woven from hazel sticks, and planted in the rocks. Shell-fish gathered from the beaches also played a part in their diet. There was a rich supply of mussels, cockle, limpets and razor fish. Limpets are still eaten and one islander gathers them from the beaches of the north end and sells them on the mainland. Hugh Miller describes being given razor fish on Eigg by a man who 'had gone to the ebb in our special behalf, and had spent a tide in laboriously filling the pail with these "treasures hid in the sand"'. On Eigg they were called the 'sprint fish' because 'they sprint out of the beach and you had to be quick to catch them'. They were collected at full moon in springtime and the islanders used to descend to Kildonnan beach and put a little salt where they were seen. 'You cooked them by pouring boiling water over the fish; if you boiled them too long they got tough. They were quite good,' says Duncan MacKay.

Trout were extracted from the burns by damming the water with large quantities of heath, stripped of its softer leaves, and tied loosely in

Duncan Mackay and his sister, Kitty Anne

bundles. These were then laid across the stream on a little mound with the tops turned upwards to the current and held down by stones. The water rose for a foot or eighteen inches against the mound. A party of islanders then went down the stream beating the banks and pools until the thickening shoal of trout, reaching the dam, would dart forward to shelter in the heath and become stuck among the branches. The stones were then quickly thrown off, the bundles tossed ashore, the better fish caught and the young fry returned to the stream.

When crops failed, which could happen after a wet summer, or supplies were exhausted after an extended winter, the people eked out their diet with other forms of food. Soup was made from nettles and several kinds of seaweed were consumed, particularly carrageen. The roots of silverweed, a yellow-flowered plant that creeps on shingle beaches, were also collected. They are full of nutrition and were dried and stored for winter use.

On Eigg they also ate numerous seabirds, particularly the shearwater, cormorant and puffin. 'Then,' says Duncan MacKay, 'they were living off the sea. But now I wouldn't kill a bird for anything'. The shearwater was consumed in such large quantities that the people of Eigg gained the nickname of 'Falach' which is the Gaelic name for the bird. The shearwaters arrived around the 17th March, made their nests in burrows on the cliffs above Cleadale and, in May, the crofters would shin up the cliffs, reach into the burrows and take the young. Being rather oily birds they were skinned rather than plucked and then boiled 'like haggis'. There are now only about one hundred pairs of shearwaters left in Eigg; rats, otters and human beings being responsible for their destruction. They were also salted down and stewed for winter food which was said to taste like veal. Only a few cormorants were eaten as they were considered too oily to be really good. They were called 'scarters'. The puffin also formed a staple part of their diet. Until about 1934 several hundred nested at Grulin but by 1953 they had all but disappeared. The young were taken from their cliff-side nests. According to Hugh Miller 'the people of Eigg, taught by their necessities, were bold cragsmen. But men do not peril life and limb for the mere sake of a meal . . . the introduction of the potato has done much to put out the practice of climbing for the bird, except among a few young lads, who find excitement enough in the work to pursue it for its own sake, as an amusement'. Fulmars, which now breed on the north-west cliffs, were also eaten. Their numbers have risen since St Kilda was evacuated in 1963 as they are no longer being caught there for food.

Rabbits were the only wild animal that was eaten. They were introduced by the Clanranald in the 18th century expressly to provide a source of food in the islands. At the beginning of this century thousands of rabbits on Eigg were trapped for export. Every year five trappers worked steadily throughout the winter laying snares on hill tracks. Some small stone shelters in the hills were built by the trappers and here they 'took their tea at dinner time if it was wet'. They each took about 2,000 pairs a year and every week the gamekeeper collected the rabbits and an estate man took them over by puffer to the mainland. Once a year, at the end of November, the trapping rights were distributed. Each trapper had his own territory, divided between Kildonnan, Laig and Howlin. 'It was winter work for the crofters and a great help as it earned extra money,' says Duncan MacKay, 'but that is all gone now, myxomatosis has killed most of the population and there are few rabbits to be seen'.

LIVING

The people of Eigg lived in 'long houses' of a type also found on Skye. They were built to withstand the severe weather and forceful gales and gave warmth and shelter to a people whose lives were mostly spent in the open air, who had few possessions and were accustomed to living close together. To the outsider they seemed dirty and dark but to the inhabitants they were all they knew and all they could construct from the local materials available.

The crofts on Eigg were built with any suitable stone or rock found on the hill or plundered from an abandoned cottage. Some of the stones were chipped into shape but most, being rounded, did not need treatment. They had short walls with rounded corners to fend off the wind and an outer and inner wall, the space between being filled with rubble. Wooden beams held up the thatched roof of rushes of which there were plenty on Eigg. Early houses had turf roofs and also enclosed a byre and a stable and each had a stone enclosure in the corner of the living room for twinning lambs. 'If you got a dead lamb you took off its skin and put it on a twin to make its new mother adopt it'. The whole family joined together to build the house which could take quite some time. Temporary shelters were sometimes 'slapped up' for a young married couple who would later get a proper house.

Formerly the crofts were built in a circle of four round the fields. This pattern can be seen in the ruins at Grulin. Each family built one wall and then joined together to build the march fence. The larger stones were used to make the walls round arable fields, necessary to protect the crops from the cattle.

At the end of the 19th century a particular type of cottage, already familiar on the mainland for a hundred years, began to be built on Eigg. These had two rooms with an attic, a slate roof and a concrete floor. They were cemented with lime collected from a seam at Cleadale, burnt in a kiln by Laig beach. Lawrence Thompson introduced the new design and they were constructed by builders from the mainland. Five stand above the road at Cuagach. The old houses below the road became the farm steadings. The new residences were considered 'palaces' to their inhabitants. Other crofters modified their old crofts, building up the side walls by about three feet and roofing them with sacking, felt, and corrugated iron and adding windows.

The fire formed the heart of the houses. It was placed in the middle of the floor and a hole in the roof provided an outlet for the smoke. The last one like this on Eigg was abandoned in about 1937. The fire gave light as well as heat. It was believed to have mystical properties and was never allowed to go out. Each evening the ashes were drawn over the embers to keep them glowing until morning when they were blown into flame. This process, called 'smooring', was only possible with smouldering peat and there were special prayers associated with the activity.

PEAT-FIRE SMOORING PRAYER

Smoor the fire, Smoor the fire,
Smoor the fire, as wanes the cruis-keen;
Jesu, guide us through the sleep-land,
Smoor the fire, Smoor the fire,
Jesu Lord, and drown wi tears
Fires o' rage where sleep lies wounded,
Fires o' rage where sleep lies wounded,
Raging fires, Raging fires,
God the Father, guard my child,
Where meet swords, where death is keening,
Hear my cry! Hear my cry!
Mary Mother, hear my cry!
On thy knee a child was cooing,
On thy knee a child was cooing,
Hear my cry! Hear my cry!
Arm o' smiting, Sword o' wounding,
Stay thou the hand, stay thou the wound,
Mary, hear a mother's prayer.

Eigg was always self-sufficient in peat, unlike some of the other islands. They were dug from the Blar Dubh moor on the road to Cleadale, by the lochan above Laig and on the Scurr ridge. Ponies carried the peats home in panniers. The process lasted four or five days each year as the round trip was ten miles and took a day. After Thompson bought Eigg in 1893 and provided paying work the islanders gradually stopped digging peats and imported coal, ending the habit altogether around 1940.

When the fire was in the middle of the room cooking was done in iron pots suspended by a chain from the ceiling or placed directly on the fire. Everything they cooked in, the pots, kettles and griddle, was made of iron. The doctor used to say that was why they were so healthy as a certain amount of iron got into everything they boiled in an iron kettle. The other utensils were made of wood or horn, until china was introduced in the 19th century, while baskets were woven from hazel twigs. 'We were well fed,' says Duncan MacKay. 'Every woman would make dishes from oats, fish and tatties. The young ones now only know how to open a tin. A lady doctor who was here called the tin-opener "the article of destruction"'.

Light not provided by the fire came from candles. Everyone made their own from sheep's tallow which was poured into moulds made from reed grass. In this century paraffin lights came in followed by tilley lamps, gas and finally, around 1951, 'the electric'. When the first cable was laid to one islander's house, in their enthusiasm everything was turned on and, at three in the morning, it melted.

All the crofters' furniture was made on the island, constructed from driftwood or anything else that came to hand. In the 19th century there was a joiner who lived at the mill and he made their chairs, benches and box beds.

The cloth for clothes and bedding was formerly made on Eigg. Everyone in each household took a hand in the process. First the sheep were shorn, then the wool was carded into 'rolags', spun, dyed with plants or lichen from the rocks and finally woven into cloth. This was then subjected to the ancient rite of 'waulking'. On the islands it was done by hand and became a ritual that astonished outside observers. About ten women took part, sitting either on the ground or across a table. The cloth, which had already been soaked in urine kept in a barrel for this purpose, was passed sunwise round the table and, at the same time, worked forwards and backwards, rubbed and thumped. This pummelling was accompanied by wild singing which started slowly and worked up to a frenzied crescendo. There are many waulking songs and this one comes from Eigg.

Croft at Cleadale

Ho mo lennan! Hey mo lennan!
Ho mo lennan! my new wooer.
Ho mo lennan! Hey mo lennan!
Cries my sweet-heart Gille Calum,
"Steersman of the 'Oak' am I".

He, mo lennan, seaman darling,
Climbeth to the mast top high.
Running up sea to the wind-wards,
Running down with a side-lie.
Sweet-heart mine, the youthful frolic,
Hard should I his love put by.

He mo lennan! Hey mo lennan
Shay mo lennan a fer oor
Ho mo lennan! Hey mo lennan
Sorror take them, those young sweet-hearts
Some of them are shy and sly.

Others come with clank and music,
Full of luring, while we're nigh.
I advise you all young lasses,
Keep three sweet-hearts to your eye,
And if one of them forsake you,
Two for you still hopeful sigh.

The islanders gradually gave up making their own cloth and the wool was sent to Brora and Inverness, returning as blankets. Those made from cheviot wool were the finest and softest. They were cheap as payment was made partly in money and partly in kind; the weaver keeping some of the wool. Their tweed was made in the Borders and it was then taken to the island tailor to be made into suits. Eigg had no special tweed of its own, the pattern depended on who was doing the weaving. The children's clothes were made at home as were everyone's knitted jumpers and stockings.

Boots were also of local manufacture. Hugh Miller gives an elaborate description of how a pair presented to him were constructed: 'They were all around a deep madder-red colour, soles, welts, and uppers and . . . were sewed not unskilfully with thongs; and their peculiar style of tie seemed of a kind suited to furnish with new idea a fashionable shoemaker of the metropolis. They were altogether the production of Eigg, from the skin out of which they had been cut, with the lime that had prepared it for the tan, and the root by which the tan had been furnished, down to the last of which they had been moulded, and the artizan that had cast them off, a pair of finished shoes. There are few trees, and, of course, no bark to spare, in the island; but the islanders find a substitute in the astringent lobiferous root of the Tormentialla Erecta, which they dig out for the purpose among the heath, at no inconsiderable expense of the time and trouble . . . the infusion of root had to be thrice changed for every skin, and that it took a man nearly a day to gather roots enough for a single infusion. I was further informed that it was not unusual for the owner of a skin to give it to some neighbour to tan, and that, the process finished, it was divided equally between them, the time and trouble bestowed on it by the one being deemed equivalent to the property held in it by the other.'

CRAFTSMEN

The community of Eigg was, until the 1st World War, largely self-sufficient. People grew their own food and various craftsmen supplied other needs. During the latter half of the 19th century, a shoemaker, tailor, carpenter, miller, merchant, grocer, boat-builder, blacksmith, wheelwright and distiller all worked on Eigg. Some of these craftsmen travelled the islands, spending time on each, while others stayed put and even combined several crafts.

At one time there were two resident tailors and 'If you wanted anything, you took them the tweed'. But, by the late 19th century, there seems to have been only one who made the rounds of the Small Isles. He was called 'Allen the tailor' and went from house to house making suits for which he charged £1 but you had to keep him as well. The Highlanders' clothes were always made by professional tailors while everything else was achieved at home. This pride in appearance is remarked on by many people and, in the 18th century, General David Stewart said that 'the Highlander will willingly submit to the plainest food and accommodation in order to procure arms and behilments which may set off to advantage a person'.

The wheelwright, who had the reputation for being the best in the west, was also the miller at the end of the 19th century. The islanders used to take their corn to the mill to be ground into meal. Payment was in kind, the miller keeping one-tenth because, according to Duncan MacKay, 'the crofters hadn't much money to pay so he was helping himself'. The mill, which still stands complete with its machinery at the bottom of Kildonnan brae, also acted as the local change or public house. Although they sold whisky there the drink was made elsewhere. Householders were allowed to make as much 'aqua vitae' as they required until, in the 18th century, levies were imposed which made smuggling profitable and illicit stills flourished. Reports indicate that the Highlanders drank whisky in huge amounts; their consumption caused a French traveller, Louis Simond, to remark 'that a Highlander would drink a quart a day and that to be able to bear that quantity of spirits he must have practised much and often'.

On Eigg the MacQuarries of Cleadale held the monopoly of distilling whisky. They altered the course of the burn so that it ran through a cave at a place called Uamh a' Bhriuthais and here they kept a still whose 'black pot' MacQuarrie and the blacksmith had walked to Inverness to fetch. Many stories are told on Eigg of how the Mac-Quarries outwitted the excisemen searching for the still. On one such occasion an exciseman arrived and did not say who he was but just that he wanted to visit the MacQuarrie's house. The islanders smelt a rat, the word went round and MacQuarrie hid the still under a tussock. When the exciseman arrived Neil MacQuarrie said he could search the house and barn. Finding nothing, he came out and found Neil standing on the tussock. With great verve Neil offered him a dram which the exciseman accepted 'and there he was standing on top of the cask and taking a dram and knowing nothing about it.'

Another time when the exciseman came to the house Neil hid the whisky in his wife's bed. She was lying there having given birth to a child two days before. Needless to say the exciseman did not investigate this place. However, these ruses did not altogether deceive the law and, 'as the net was closing', Neil MacQuarrie stopped his trade.

The blacksmith was also permanently resident on Eigg. Iron bars were brought from the mainland and fashioned into whatever was required for the farm and house from horse-shoes to ploughs and cooking pots. The smithy stands above the pier and the forge was traditionally worked by the Campbell family. Donald Campbell, who still lives on Eigg and worked for the estate, is the great grandson of the original blacksmith. The smith was an important member of the old crofting communities; as recognition of his special skills he often appears in old folk-tales. In the days of the clans the office was generally hereditary and he made all the chain mail shirts, dirks and sword blades. When clan warfare came to an end his importance declined. He found other work shoeing horses and making metal implements for agriculture. Iron was expensive; a person's wealth was often indicated by the amount he possessed and some thought it had magical properties. This was especially true of the chains from which hung the cauldron type of cooking pots. They were all different and it was associated with the powers of evil. Children were not allowed to touch it and bits of firewood were often stuck in its links to prevent fairies climbing down the chimney.

The boat-builder lived at Cleadale. Every crofter had a craft which, when not in use, was pulled up from the shore and sat outside his front gate. Many were very primitive. The seams were caulked with moss steeped in tar, the hawsers and rigging ropes made of twisted tree roots and the sails were locally woven from cloth of a harder and stouter kind than that used for plaids. The one square, woollen sail or 'lug' was fairly useless unless the wind was blowing in the right direction and, as a result, they mainly relied on oars to get them through the water. The boats were strongly built for rough trade and those used for transporting cattle were fitted with barriers which prevented the animals from falling in rough seas for 'a fallen beast in a crowded boat seldom got up'.

Water has always played a great part in Highland life as a means of defence and as transport, especially before there were roads, and for fishing. Tales of loss at sea abound and special prayers were recited by the steersmen with responses from the crew before a voyage. Rowing songs lightened the labour. John Know, travelling through the Highlands in 1787, describes how his crew, pulling in the teeth of an adverse wind, sang 'in choruses observing a kind of time with the movement of the oars'.

THE SHIP THAT SAILETH HOME

Love that wanders give no heart to,
Hee ree o ha-lo-ve
Ebb and flow of waters yon love,
He-ro heeo, how-lo ha lo vee, lew rova hoo-a
Love that loves thy cattle, hear not,
Heeree o halovee,
Wind from Northland, cold wi' snow yon,
Ho ro hee o howlo halovee lew-ro-va hoo-a
Love that trembles give no wound to,
Hee-ree o ha-lo-vee,
Yons the ship that saileth home-ward,
Ho ro hee o, how-lo ha-lo-vee, lew ro va hoo-a.

THE BIRLINN OF THE WHITE SHOULDERS

A Clanranald Seaman's love song to his boat

Out at sea, Fair is she,
Fairer than the Dame Clanranald,
Fairer than she!
Not a wave in straits or narrows
But is glad when she is coming
Out to sea! Fair is she,
Fairer than the Dame Clanranald,
Fairer than she!
Out to sea fareth she,
White her shoulders cresting sea foam,
Far fareth she,
Out to Uist and out to Lewis,
And outward bound to Rodel in Harris,
Fareth she, Out to sea,
White her shoulders cresting sea-foam,
Far fareth she!
Out at sea fairest she,
White her shoulders cresting sea-foam,
Fairest is she!
Not a seal or brindled sea-duck,
But would fain be following after
Out to sea! Fairest she,
Fairer than the Dame Clanranald,
Fairer than she!

MYTHS, SONGS AND FESTIVALS

Today, the old customs and folk beliefs have virtually disappeared and enquiries are dismissed with the words, 'It used to be so in the old days, but it does not happen now' or 'the old people used to say it'. However, Kenneth MacLeod, writing in 1909, remarked that the island 'remained a nest of antique Celticism'.

One common belief which persisted in the Highlands was that before someone was to die an old lady would be seen by certain burns washing their shroud. On Eigg she was to be found beside the burn on the Bealach Clithe brae leading down to Cleadale. Here there is a green spot by the stream bank above the road which was the favourite haunt of the little lady. She lived long ago, in a place whose whereabouts nobody knew, and wore a green dress and was always washing clothes 'as hard as her two little elbows would go'. They called her the Washerwoman and it was not known if she was one of the fairies or why she was always washing. On one occasion she was spoken to by 'an over-bold, over-inquisitive islander, curious to know whose shroud she was preparing'. She 'more than satisfied his curiosity by telling him it was his own'.

The islanders thought the seals who crooned in the reefs were women transformed. They were regarded as the children of the King of Lochlann or Wonderland beyond the seas – 'You could tell by the very eyes that there is kingly blood in them'. There are many variations on the story of the seal-woman who, adopting human form, captures the heart and is married by a mortal man. He then suffers deep anguish when she returns to the sea which she must, 'Three times a year when the full moon is brightest'.

THE SEAL-WOMAN'S CROON

Pillow'd on the sea-wrack brown am I
On the gleaming white sheen sand, o hi
Lulled by sweet croon of waves I lie
Could slumber deep – part thee and me.

Far a-way my own *gruagach* lone
On the gleaming white friend reefs o hi
Lies, and that the cause of all my moan,
Did slumber deep – part thee and me.

On the morrow shall I o'er the Sound
Oe'r the gleaming white sheen sand, oh hi
Swim until I reach my *grah-yan down*,
                   [loved one brown]
Nor slumber deep – part thee and me.

Mrs Kennedy Fraser puts forward the theory in *Songs of the Hebrides* that the Isles-folk learned songs from the seals. She bases this on an instance when she and a party of friends were resting on the sands in Barra beyond which ran a long line of skerries where innumerable great grey seals basked in the sun. As an experiment she began singing the Sea-woman's Sea-joy 'in the most carrying tone I could summon . . . Instantly the response began at the southern end of the reef, and a perfect fusillade of single answering tones came from seal after seal, travelling rapidly northward, until at the further end of the reef it ceased. Then, after a moment of intense silence, a beautiful solo voice sang a phrase . . . The voice was quite human in character but much greater in volume than any mezzo-soprano I have ever heard . . . Is the song I sang really a seal song . . . or did the Isles-folk learn it from the seals'.

All animals were revered because it was believed that, before the Fall, they had the power of speech and from their superior innocence could see much that is invisible to men not gifted with the second sight. Many visionary stories and warnings make use of this unique faculty. Because animals shared in the Fall they will also share in the Redemption, while horses can communicate with departed spirits. Cows were especially holy and given extra food at certain festivals.

Birds, too, were attributed with Christ-like qualities, particularly white birds. Seagulls were regarded as carriers between the land-under-the-waves and the land-of-the-living. Seeing a swan was a good omen, but seeing seven, or a multiple of seven, ensured peace and prosperity for the equivalent number of years. Hearing a swan in the morning, especially on Tuesday, was much to be desired. Swans were sacred because, it was said, long ago before the days of the Red Flood the moon shone with such brightness you could see the bristles on a man's foot by its light. This put great anger on the sun as he lay on his back in the Outer Sea. 'I will arise,' said the sun, 'and outshine you shameless moon.' He arose and ever since the moon is paler than she should be, except when the ripening corn puts a glow on her face. Her daughter, the wild swan, is stately and silent under the sun but sweet-voiced, even if sad, under the moon.

Kenneth MacLeod who tells the story also recorded this song on Eigg.

Swan of the West,
Mate of my heart,
Westward I'd fly toward Jura.

On night of stars
Strangewards I'd fly,
Westward fly toward Jura.

Swan of the West
Mate of my heart
Would that with thee toward Jura.

On night of stars,
Far might I fly,
Westward fly toward Jura.

On Eigg they sometimes call the oyster-catcher St Donnan's bird, and say the saint gave the bird its distinctive black and white colours. But here, and in other parts of the Isles, it is also called St Bride's bird and they tell that one day Christ was sitting on a skerry in the ebb-tide when through a mountain pass came His enemies. The oyster-catcher, seeing them, said 'Yon shall not be; I will put wandering on the evil men' and went and covered his Lord with sea-weed. In remembrance of this deed, when St Michael was made warden of the sea, he decided to 'put the whiteness of an angel on the oyster-catcher'. But St Bride, foster-mother of Christ, made the suggestion that 'the bird that saved my Child be just as He was, but with a touch of whiteness on him, for remembrance'. It was placed in the shape of the cross and ever since, when the oyster-catcher is on the wing, 'the touch of whiteness on him, as of an angel, is seen of all eyes, as though a cross'. St Bride's bird, being the servant of the foster-mother Mary, keeps a warm eye on all little children and did so in this story told on Eigg:

One day, long ago, three little motherless children were playing on the white sands of Laig Bay, long after the other little ones of the township had been mothered to sleep. As they played one of the three espied a coracle tied to a rock. 'Her prow to the sea!' cried the little one, 'let's now play at being sea-reivers', and climbing into the coracle they set her adrift on the out-going tide while singing bold reiving songs. But as midnight drew near and the giant hills of Rhum loomed over them the reiver heart oozed out, and the child heart throbbed with fear. But the warm eye was not asleep; quietly over the waves came Bride answering the call of her seabird and, from an armful of the moorland cannach, she took the soft white tufts and made a bed for the motherless three and guided the coracle on the inflowing tide back to Laig, lulling the children to sleep with a croon.

Aspen trees were planted by the side of houses because on Eigg they held that there is more wisdom in the bird-world than in the folk-world. Men fling their curses at the aspen tree because the Cross was made from its wood but birds nest in its branches knowing it could not help the shame of this deed for which it has trembled ever since 'in all its leaves'.

CURSE OF THE ASPEN TREE

A curse on thee thou aspen tree,
The King o' Bens was nailed to thee,
Upon the balde a black curse be,
And on his hand who set it free.

A curse on thee hard aspen tree,
The King o' grace was nailed to thee,
The love of men and angels he
Whose blood flowed down from yonder tree.

A curse on thee, thou aspen tree,
A curse that thou should'st ever be,
A curse on whoso may see
And will not curse with me yon tree.

Some of the more potent myths were attached to the sea. 'The sounds of the Western Sea are aye such as can be "understanded" of the folk. They foretell good weather and bad, birth and death in the township, the drowning of dear ones on faraway shores. In the storm they voice the majesty of the King of the Elements, and in the quiet evening they fill one with a longing which is hope born of pain. Perhaps other seas have voices for other folk, but the Western Sea alone can speak in the Gaelic tongue and reach the Gaelic heart. To an Islesman the German Ocean, for instance, seems cold and dumb, a mere mass of water seasoned with salt; it has no mermaids and no second-sight, and if it has seals, they are not the children of the King of Lochlann. To one sea only, does the old Gaelic by-word apply: "The sea invites acquaintance."

'The Western Sea, as every Isles man knows, can, even on a quiet evening, laugh like a youth whose love-tale is running smoothly, and moan like an aged man bewailing the sins of the past; both the laugh and the moan, however, are the children of the *atmosphere*, rather than of the sea itself.

'The fisher-crofters, who get their living from the sea' had a 'life-long struggle with something greater than themselves.' They are fully alive to its seduction and its cruelty. 'The sea,' says Kenneth MacLeod, 'has cast her spell upon the impressionable Celt – her generosity, her might, her playfulness, her frequent cruelty, are felt, but what really haunts the Celtic mind is her awful mysteriousness.'

For the women the loss by drowning of a husband, brother or lover was all too frequent an occurrence. Some claimed that the sounds of the Singing Sands were the voices of men drowned at sea and that those who remained for a night alone on the beach could talk to their dead. 'Little Eigg was very much a sea island and reputed to know the sea's will. The sea did not like excessive sorrowing for those who were drowned; indeed it was well known that a lament should not be sung twice in one night; it would anger the sea and be dangerous. But Eigg went further and claimed that "every tear a woman lets fall for one she loved will fall on him beneath the sea as a drop of blood" and he might even be drowned twice, once in water and once in blood.' These chilling lines are from a song called the Sea-Sorrow:

The spirits of the drowned did not share this gloomy picture. A woman who once asked the spirit of her drowned husband, 'Cold thy bed tonight?' was answered, 'It is neither hot nor cold, but just as one might wish, if as he wished he got.' His wife then suggested, 'If not cold, lonely at any rate', and got the reply, 'I have the best heroes of Lochlann beside me, and the best bards of Erin, and the best story-tellers of Alba, and what we do not know ourselves, the seal and the swan tell us.' The woman then said, 'Treasure of my heart, are not we the foolish ones to be weeping and sorrowing for the men, and they so happy in the land-under-waves'. 'Thou speakest truth there,' said the man and vanished into the night and under the sea.

Stories were told in which the spirits of the drowned men, exasperated beyond all patience, appear in their old homes, between midnight and cock-crow, giving their women such a fright it dries their tears and banishes their sorrow. In the Hebrides an excess of joy or grief is regarded as tempting Providence and it was often said that 'laughing over much is an omen of tears, and weeping over much an omen of greater evil to come'.

The sea has given the Hebridean song 'its fiercest joy and most passionate sorrow'. The sad ones are most numerous and generally sung by women who have lost husband, brother and sweetheart. Rapturous songs are fewer and invariably belong to men who 'reive and rove, and dream of strange lands and adventures beyond the waves.'

Cold, cold, cold,
Cold, the sea and snakish,
Cold, cold, cold,
From depth to top-wave, she.

SEA-KEENING SONG

Never boat comes – Round yon headland
But that ever – Flame my pale cheeks.

Never ship comes – Thro' the narrows
But sudden – Change I colour.

I am a woman – Under sorrow
On a bare knoll – Bare, and cold.

Lonely is – Thy pillow
In thy chamber – Up yonder.

How care I – E'er to smooth it
And thou so – Far from me.

Ah, my wound – Soft they brown curls
Sea-tossed – Sea-torn.

THE REIVING SHIP

Early sails she to the reiving
Flashing by the frowning headlands
Early sails she to the reiving
Grinds beneath her, grey-blue limpets.
Crunches curving whelks to sand-drift.

Early sails she to the reiving
Sweeps she gaily Moola's waters
Kyles and Moyles to fair green Isla,
Leaps her way to Isles of daring,
Gleaming Isles of blades and laughter.

A ho hi to Isles of daring
In the dawn she goes a reiving a ho hi

The wreck of the Puffer: The Jenny of Glasgow

'Only those whose ears have been filled for weeks and days together with the moan of the sea, and of the wind round one of those rocky isles can realise how much there is of their haunting mystery reflected in the music of the race.'

The songs the Highlanders composed are outstanding and encompassed every occasion. There were love songs, humorous songs, laments and working songs. The latter accompanied all forms of work helping the people through their endless, uniform tasks; rowing, weaving, winding the quern, gathering in the harvest. The sound of singing can never have been absent. Boswell says in his *Tour of the Hebrides*, how, as they landed at Raasay 'the music of the rowers was succeeded by that of the reapers'. Kenneth MacLeod describes how the songs were 'almost invariably long, consisting often of many verses strung on strongly characteristic recurrent refrains. They were intended, in the case of working songs, to carry one over long stretches of monotonous labour. To this end it was essential that they should have an inherent *circular* quality; that they should tend to turn over upon themselves; that they should appear to end, not at the end but at the beginning; that the last note, contrary to custom, should in its very nature be unrestful and onward-driving, carrying the singer perforce to the inevitable repetition. . . . I have seen the islanders while singing them seem to get hypnotised with their own rhythm, working themselves into a frenzy with it, and no one who has not witnessed it can realise what an intoxicating power strong rhythm can exercise over the Celtic temperament.'

Songs were also sung at ceilidhs. These were the centre of social life for the old communities. It was for the ceilidh that the old rhymes were made and where the bards recited their poems and satires and preserved the tales of Ossian, Fingal,

Graine and Cuchullin. And it was for the ceilidh that the people strung together the legends of their island homes so that every hill, loch and glen has its own traditions. The people were intensely creative. Every cottage had a musician and every township a poet. The people would gather together during the winter evenings and the man of the house would take the lead and tell the first tale. Everyone else was expected to follow with a story, personal anecdote, riddle or saying. Discussions of all kinds took place from the practical to the supernatural and sometimes there was singing, playing of the fiddle and dancing as well.

Kenneth MacLeod says that in his youth 'at the ceilidh, the folk told the tales and sang the ballads of the Fayne, or of the less-ancient heroes, the Lord of the Isles, MacLeod of Dunvegan, and "our own treasure, Clanranald" – with, for Sundays and holy days, beautiful legends of Iona and Oronsay. But whether on holy or other eve, as midnight drew nearer, the tales and the songs, and the distant roar of the Western Sea grew weirder, until at last song and tale ceased, and the fire smouldered, and the cruisie-light flickered, and the folk whispered, while over the ceilidh crept the shadow of night and the mysteries hiding therein. "Sweet is the lark at dawn," said the Eigg folk, "but sweeter the cock at midnight."'

Angus MacKinnon, speaking of the ceilidhs of his childhood, recounts that, 'in those days, one took place every night, but not on a big scale. The winter day was short. It was dark about 3.30 and didn't get light again until 9 or 9.30 a.m. So it was a short day but a long night and there was plenty of time for cards, telling yarns and singing songs. That is the way they used to spend their evenings. The women used to knit while the men yarned. They could go back for generations. My whole family were great traditionalists. So if the youngsters were around they heard those stories, time and time and time again. That is how tradition lives. There was no electric light, no television, no papers and there were more people then, more life, more parties and gatherings'. Sometimes ceilidhs were more elaborate then, there 'was dancing, then a break and somebody sang a song, then some more dancing. That was the way it went. They liked the songs whether they could sing or not. My father couldn't sing but he loved the songs and a lot of the ladies could sing'.

A dancing master used to come and teach the children, giving lessons in the school every week. 'They could dance far better than now,' says Duncan MacKay. 'They can hardly do the Scottish dances now. It is more like a disco.' The music was supplied by the pipe and fiddle and, in later years, the accordion. At weddings and balls the people of Eigg danced the Dansa Mor. This was originally a tribal dance and came from Skye. It was introduced to Eigg at the turn of the century by two men who went to Rhum to help build the Bullough's castle. 'There were some men from Skye also helping and they had this dance. The Big Dance they called it. It was danced before a battle and only performed by men. There was no music, instead they were reciting themselves. Any number could take part but it was usually ten or twelve men and they were dancing in a circle, with hopping steps. Two men would go into the middle of the circle and sing verses to each other and it was always the same two men.' Lawrence Thompson christened it the Eigg War Dance, he wanted to see it and the islanders gave a special

performance in the school-house. There was a doctor from Newfoundland present and he was going round saying 'Are the men mad'.

Christmas and New Year were also celebrated by dances. Easter was marked by the young people taking picnics into the hills. They were 'taking eggs and scones and other home-made things and often going as far as Grulin, making a fire and boiling eggs in tins. It was great sport. We were eating half a dozen at a time and chatting'. At Hallowe'en they used to dress up and get up to all sorts of tricks; 'stuffing people's chimneys so that all the smoke came down into the room, locking doors and letting the horses free'.

A traditional game of shinty was played five times a year: at Christmas, on New Year's Day, called by them Three Kings Day after the three wise men, All Hallows, St Andrew's Day and Epiphany. Hugh MacKinnon recounts how everybody on the island used to gather on Laig beach at about 12 o'clock. Two young lads were then chosen to pick sides. When everyone was divided the two lads would throw their stick or 'caman' into the air and the direction the teams played in was decided according to how the fore-hand fell. You went to the south side if your caman fell with the forehand facing north. The goals were marked by rocks and set about 12 feet apart. There was no fixed distance between the goals but they were probably about 200 yards apart.

There were about twenty to thirty players on each side and the game kept going until about three in the afternoon, unless the tide stopped them, but they often played on when 'they hadn't much more width left than three or four yards of beach'. If the tide allowed they would stay 'till night had fallen and the stars were in the sky . . . and they would be so tired they couldn't sup milk

from a spoon. But they were drinking before they went down to play and there were times when that wasn't the best for either. They would be going the rounds of the houses and some of them, depending on their temperament, would find it easier to pick a fight because they were having drams. Not that I saw much in the way of fighting.' Once, an old man of eighty was playing, with not a stitch on but his trousers and shirt. Someone hit a ball from the other side, 'he saw it coming and it was about chest high and he stuck out his chest and stopped the ball. Ah, the poor man, I think he died the next summer'.

They had their own rules but no one refereed the play. There were various ways to score goals but none counted unless the ball was running along the ground or anyway a few inches above the ground. The ball was a lump of hazel-root. It was whittled into shape with a knife, smoothed with a rasp or file and then toughened by being boiled in water. 'I can assure you, if you were hit by those balls you would feel it.' The camans were cut in the woods from hazel, elm, oak, willow or birch. Elm and birch made fine, light camans but were easily broken, oak was the hardest, strongest and most durable but often gave 'a sting' through the shaft as you hit the ball. The sticks were four feet long, whittled into shape, heated in a peat fire and bent in a clamp for two days.

Children were not allowed to play with the men until they were fourteen. They had a game of their own on a separate part of the beach. After about 1925 they gradually stopped playing shinty and turned to football and this is the game played by the island men today.

Christenings, marriages and deaths, ceremonies that are the landmark of most people's lives, were all observed in special ways by the people of Eigg.

When a baby was christened, if it was Catholic it was taken to the chapel, but if Protestant then the minister came to the house to perform the ceremony.

Weddings went on for days. 'They used to have great weddings here', says Duncan MacKay, 'they were going on for three days and it was mostly in the houses.' After the church service they repaired to the bride's house where the people sat and chatted and were given food. In small houses they could not take all the guests at once so first there was a party for the relations, then the old people came and so on until everyone had been entertained. The guests supplied all the food; 'they were cooking stuff and taking it round in relays so that everybody would have something.

The bridegroom just had to buy the whisky'. Some of the larger wedding receptions were held in the steadings at Kildonnan and Laig. After the church service they all repaired here for a grand ceilidh.

The rituals connected with death have always played an important part in the Highlands. They have a freedom from the fear of death attributed to their sense of the continuity of family, clan and history. Evidence of this can be seen in the strong desire among Highland people to be buried 'with their own' and people are carried huge distances often from far-flung parts of the mainland, back to the family burial ground. Death croons, recited over the dying, are part of their poetry.

Home thou art going tonight to the Winter
The Autumn, Summer, and Spring-tide
Everhouse Home art going tonight on music of cantors,
White angels thee wait on the shores of the Avon
God the Father with thee in sleep,
Jesus Christ with thee in Sleep,
God the Spirit with thee in sleep
Softly sleep, Softly sleep.
Sleep oh love on mother's bosom,
Sleep while she sings soft lullings to thee,
The sleep of the Son on Mary's bosom,
Sleep and put off from thee every woe,
Sleep and put off from thee every woe,
Sleep and put off from thee every woe.

Once dead, the body lay in the parlour and friends and neighbours took it in turns to keep it company. It was an obligatory sign of respect for everyone round about to visit the corpse. On Eigg all the men dig the grave. They descend to Kildonnan Churchyard, a plot is selected and the turf rolled back on a stick. Digging then commences but, because of the rocky ground, the grave is often rather shallow and the term 'six feet under' does not apply here. Sometimes, owing to the lack of gravestones, confusions arise, and a new site has to be sought. No invitations are issued for the funeral but it is customary for all to attend. After the church ceremony the coffin is carried to the graveyard and Catholics are paraded in a sun-wise direction once round the old church before being laid in the grave. This was sometimes marked with a rock but usually they 'just did not bother, but they kept a plan of where everybody was buried'. They are all numbered and each relates to a person. Today most graves have a stone.

PROSPEROUS TIMES
FOR EIGG

In 1893 the MacPherson family sold Eigg to Robert Lawrence Thompson MacEwen, a mysterious man whose origins and motives for buying the island were the subject of endless speculation. What appears definite is that he was the son of a John MacEwen of Inverness but, at some point, decided to drop his first and last names and call himself Lawrence Thompson. He began his career as foreign correspondent of *The Times* but later became an agent for Vickers, the armament sup-

pliers, and began selling weapons to the revolution in Chile and Peru. He may have fought with the rebels, as there is a story that during a raid he sacked a convent, brought the anger of the church down on his head, and, as a result, felt cursed for the rest of his life.

From South America Thompson moved to the Far East, sold arms to the Afghans fighting the British on the North-West Frontier and then to the Chinese in rebellion against their government. It seems likely that by now he was no longer acting as an agent for Vickers but had become an arms dealer in his own right, prepared to supply anyone with the money to pay. From China,

Thompson moved to Japan and equipped their navy with old ships bought cheaply in Britain. He became friends with the Emperor and others in the Japanese hierarchy.

Many of Thompson's methods were highly questionable and he achieved a reputation as a renegade at a time, and in countries, where adventurous piracy was the rule. It was said that he bought Eigg to escape assassins and changed his name to further confuse his pursuers. He was also supposed to have been married and was devoted to his wife but she died and, grieving, he became very reclusive. This could also have been a reason for buying a remote island.

Eigg was not Thompson's only Scottish property, he also owned Muck, Sleat of Skye and land on the mainland. Initially his estates were managed by his brother and a factor. Thompson took up residence on Eigg in 1897, choosing to arrive on Queen Victoria's Diamond Jubilee Day. To celebrate the double event, the islanders built two great bonfires, one below Galmisdale House and another on top of the Scurr. To make the latter, old boats were dragged by horse to the base of the rock, broken up and carried by men to the summit and constructed into 'a gigantic pile'. Unfortunately on the 'great day' the island was enveloped in mist and, although the fires were lit, they could not be seen.

Thompson was a man of eccentric habits and these, combined with his strange Eastern connections, soon earned him a place in island folk-lore. Stories are still told of his long, solitary walks at night and the fact that, once a year, he dined alone at a table laid for three. A room in his house was designated the 'curio room' and here he kept some weird effigies and two swords of Toledo steel in cases. The swords were to be presents, one for the commander-in-chief of the Japanese land forces and the other for the admiral of the Japanese fleet but, for some reason, they were never sent. Thompson's friend, the Emperor of Japan, was also supposed to come and stay on Eigg but he never arrived.

At first Thompson lived in the MacPhersons' lodge but, as it was enclosed by trees and had no view, he decided to move to Galmisdale. Alterations were made to the house and, to give himself peace and quiet, he moved the five crofters still living at Galmisdale to the Cuagach. A sensible idea as it concentrated all the remaining crofters at Cleadale and vastly improved the lives of those from Galmisdale. They were built new houses with concrete floors and Ballachulish slate roofs and given land. Duncan Ferguson says that 'It was only thatched houses they had at Galmisdale and the new crofts were drained and they were much better off . . . To them their new houses were like palaces compared to the hovels they had left'. They also had more land, 8 acres of arable, a small acreage round the house and 50 acres of common grazing where they could keep four cows and a horse, whereas at Galmisdale they only had enough for a couple of cows and no horse.

Other crofters were helped to improve their cottages by being given loans. Thompson took a great interest in the alterations. Duncan MacKay describes how 'Thompson was always walking round the island and when he heard of his father's plans to exchange a thatch roof for one of slate and to have a fire at each end of the cottage instead of one in "its traditional place smoking in the middle"', he came to call. 'This is a crofter's house,' he said, implying that it should remain so. However, MacKay explained that if you had a fire at each end it kept you warmer and, seeing the logic of the argument, Thompson replied, 'Oh that's a good idea, you can go ahead'. He also gave 'loans' to anyone unfortunate enough to lose a cow, the money being taken out of their earnings. 'They paid a certain amount out of every pound they earned on the Estate and when they weren't working they didn't pay.'

These improving gestures were a few of the many Thompson was to make on Eigg. His Eastern deeds had made him a fortune, estimated in those days to be a quarter of a million, and he lavished the money on Eigg to the benefit of the islanders. Paying work was provided in his house and on the estate and 'Everyone on the island that could work for him did so' either full or part-time. Miles of fences were constructed, the Blar Mor at Kildonnan was drained and trees were planted. There was employment at hay and harvest time and sometimes men from Eigg were taken to work on Muck. It was a long day. They had to be at the pier by 7 am to be transported to Muck where they worked until 6 pm, landing back on Eigg around 7 pm and then had to walk the three or four miles back to Cleadale.

Thompson enjoyed the islanders' company and gave them parties at which the drink flowed. Duncan MacKay tells how after one particularly good one, Donald MacLeod, the gamekeeper, who was 'drunk all the time' called at the lodge in the morning as was his daily habit. Thompson always inquired after the weather, asking 'How's the glass today Donald, high or low?' On this morning MacLeod replied, 'Very empty Sir', and helped himself to a whisky.

Social innovations were also sponsored by Thompson. The first resident doctor was appointed in 1897. Before this the critically ill set sail for Oban, Arisaig or Sleat of Skye depending on the direction of the wind. Alternatively they could send a boat for the doctor but this was beyond the resources of the ordinary crofter and,

between 1855–97, only 12% of the deaths in the Small Isles were medically certified. The poor people mostly cured themselves using ancient remedies, some dating back to pagan times.

There was a belief that certain wells cured or predicted the outcome of an illness. The veneration for wells was so strongly ingrained that early Christian missionaries frequently accepted the fact and many, such as St Columba's Well at Cleadale, are dedicated to a saint. The well at Five Pennies and that at Tobar nam Ban Naomh were supposed to have healing properties and 'its water should not be used for tasks like washing potatoes'. The islanders believed that, if they drank a quantity of water for two or three days, it never failed to cure someone of their first disease. However, if a stranger lay by the well at night-time, it gave him a deformity in some part of his body, 'this they say hath been frequently experimented'.

The Highlanders had a reputation for uncanny powers of healing. Martin Martin says that the islanders, although denied the pursuit of conventional studies, 'seem to be versed in the book of nature than many that have greater opportunities of improvement'. They preserve their health 'by temperance and the prudent use of simples for which they first make experiments and then reason their effects'. Many of the plants they used have been proved to possess curative properties. If all else failed there was always the whisky. Goodrich Freer wrote, 'that one cannot fail to be struck, in going through the Islands, by the singular absence, even as compared with the mainland, of cripples, or blind persons, or persons of weak intellect. One obvious, though perhaps superficial explanation, lies in the theory of the survival of the fittest, in the fact that a good constitution must be needed to survive existence at all'.

Thompson invested money to provide the school-children with a daily cup of cocoa and one large biscuit from October to March. It was one of various incentives used to get the children to school. Attendance cards were given to those who came regularly and, at one time, children who were present every day in the week were allowed home half an hour early on Friday while, in winter, the school did not open until 10 am. In 1908 a visitor to the lodge left shillings at the school to be donated to the best boy and girl. In spite of these inducements, attendance was difficult to enforce. The school log-book records numerous excuses for absence of which stormy weather is the most frequent. Sometimes, when there had been a long spell of particularly bad weather there was Saturday school to make up for lost time. Farmwork, especially potato planting and harvesting, also kept children away. On October 30th, 1908, for instance, the log-book records, 'Most of the crofters have now lifted all their potatoes, so the children are able to come to school'. Illness was an important reason for absence. From January 21st to March 16th, 1908, the school was closed due to an attack of measles. Influenza and diphtheria are often mentioned as causes of closure. In 1914 it was closed for a fortnight because of diphtheria and one child died. The school also closed for the day for weddings and funerals.

At first it was not the custom to go to school and perhaps only one in a family attended. The children started at six years of age and left at fourteen. At the beginning of this century there were forty to fifty pupils in the school taught by three teachers; a primary one, a secondary one and a pupil. Lessons were generally in English although the occasional teacher from the islands did manage to squeeze a bit of Gaelic into the curriculum. 'They were good teachers,' remembers Angus MacKinnon. 'They made you write and do arithmetic and listen. We were much better educated than many that went away.' There were no school lunches and they took a piece with them, often eating it as they dallied on the way, dropping stones down the cliff hole above the sheep fank at Kildonnan until hearing the school bell. Donald Campbell was one of a family of twelve and his mother made them all hold hands so that none would stray.

After school the children helped on the croft. On the way home they would assist with the peat-cutting, stopping with the men at Blar Mor for their tea. They herded cattle in summer and winter and cut bracken for their bedding. They also helped with the ploughing. Once at home they would take a turn on the spinning wheel or the loom. Life was 'not boring at all. Everyone has their own way and theirs was a different way'.

Many of the teachers came from the south and seldom stayed long. They did not understand the island conditions and, as the Inspector's Annual Report of 1908 states, 'this created controversy between the parents and teachers and, combined with poor attendance, militated against the efficiency of the school'. One of the main disagreements was the use of Gaelic which was favoured by the parents but not the authorities. The Inspector's report continued with the words, 'it is quite evident also, that far too much use has been made of the vernacular in the teaching of the children'. Often, however, the teachers were dedicated and made great efforts to place able children in the high school on the mainland.

One in particular was dedicated to encouraging their imaginations. Iain Og Morragh, poet, musician, dancer and courtier, was schoolmaster on Eigg at the turn of the century. He was the son of a laird on Skye who spent his early years working for the Government in London. But, 'high living and a warm heart soon brought him within sight of the debtor's cell', and he escaped to Skye where he spent the next few years. Eventually friends got him appointed to the parish school on Eigg and here, 'for over a generation' he played the fiddle, composed and collected songs and taught the children 'the Spanish ambassador's deportment and the Princess Caroline's curtsey' and regaled them with stories of court life. According to one of his pupils, 'He was a treasure of a teacher, on dull or rainy days, his first words to us always were "Ye children of other folk, what brought you here today? My curse on gloom! It was ever a bad teacher – let us to the fiddle and dance". On bright sunny days he had an equally good philosophy, saying "Is it not a great sin, children of my heart, to be packed in this narrow room like puffins in a hole, while the sun is so warm and radiant outside, and the bird-world so frolicsome!" And, in a twinkling of an eye we were all out on the green grass laughing on the threshold of a beautiful day of song and dance. My thousand blessings on Iain Og Morragh . . . If he failed to make the youth of the island bad Saxons, he made them good Gaels, ready on the slightest provocation to rush into song, dance and tale.'

In 1899, anxious, perhaps, to maintain some contact with the outside world, Thompson introduced the telegraph service to Eigg. Before this, as Stanhope wrote in 1806 about Skye, difficulties of transport could mean that 'Bonaparte might easily have effected a landing and England have been long under the insulting dominion of a conqueror, before the knowledge of his departure from Paris could penetrate here'. And earlier, in 1798, the *Statistical Account* complains that 'another inconvenience arises from the want of a post office, in a proper situation, on the opposite continent. The nearest post town is Fort William. From Fort William to Ardnasouran is about 40 computed miles ... from Ardnasouran, the nearest stage to Eigg, is about 11 miles over water. A post office at Ardnasouran, and a packet between Arisaig and Uist to call at Eigg and Canna, would prove highly beneficial in facilitating the intercourse between these islands and the continent'. In 1812, when the road to Fort William was opened, a post office was established in Arisaig

but deliveries, even in the 1860s, were extremely erratic. Letters to Eigg were merely addressed to the Clerk of the Clansman Steam Packet, c/o Custom House, Greenock, for Post Master Arisaig, and their distribution was left largely to chance. Kenneth MacLeod records their progress round the Small Isles: 'A smack crossed from the Island of Eigg to the mainland once in the week, weather and inclination permitting, for the few letters and one newspaper brought by stage-coach from Fort William to Arisaig: about a fortnight later, somebody sailed across from Rhum to Eigg to see if any letters had arrived . . . in the course of another week, more or less, a shepherd from the west side of Rhum, looking for stray sheep, unexpectedly found himself in the seaport Clachan of Kinloch, and while there might remember to ask if there were any letters for the neighbouring island of Canna; on the following day the folk of Canna saw a fire on a certain hill in Rhum . . . and some time before the end of the week somebody, who probably never in his life received a letter, sailed across the Sound and returned with the mail bag as soon as he felt in the mood for returning.'

A visitor to Eigg in 1863, Packenham Edgeworth, became so frustrated by the system he resorted to desperate means, 'I have chartered a boat to go to Arisaig for letters tomorrow as I cannot stand any longer this entire silence from the rest of the world', he expostulated.

Thompson first established the post office at Laig but then, finding it too far from the lodge, moved it to Galmisdale House. However, he changed his mind again when he saw it was now too far away for the Cleadale crofters and com-

Transfer from the 'flit boat' to MacBrayne's ferry

134

promised, in 1901, by placing it in the middle of the island. It still stands here although originally it was on the other side of the road.

During 1899 the authorities began laying a telegraph line to Rhum and Canna and Thompson arranged that it should be extended to Eigg. The thick wire hawser came ashore at Laig and terminated in a small hut above the beach where it remains in a decayed state. The telephone exchange also eventually moved to the centre of the island, joining the post office. The operator used to sit in one corner of the shop manning a switchboard of twelve lines. One for each phone on the island, wound up by hand.

Communications to Eigg were further improved when, in the 1870s, steam ships began to ply regular routes round the islands making it possible to 'perform journeys in a day which a hundred years ago would have been considered the business of a week and the boast of a lifetime'. Before the 19th century few visited the Western Isles but, after the publication of Martin Martin's account and that of Boswell and Johnson, others began to come in increasing numbers, attracted by the 'mountains, minerals and scenery' of the west coast. Early travellers had an arduous journey. The Revd. Charles Lesingham Smith, Fellow of Christ's College, Cambridge, going to Skye in 1853, had to disembark from his train at Kinlochailort and walk the 12 miles to the ferry at Arisaig. Here he found the charge for the crossing was a bottle of whisky, 'currency of a certain kind' being preferred to money in these remote areas!

By the end of the century, MacBraynes had begun to claim the monopoly they now hold over ferry boats. They advertised summer tours of the Royal Route on suitably named boats: *Hakon, Robert the Bruce, Bonnie Prince Charlie* and *Queen Victoria*. For £4.00 with meals you could do a week's tour of islands, including Eigg, leaving from Glasgow. Tourists were tempted with itineraries that embraced: 'pleasant little towns where the steamer puts in for an hour or two, the clachan piers it touches at, to set a passenger or so ashore, and the island roadsteads where a boat comes out and is towed alongside for the few moments in the clear green seas, while the mails are taken on board. There is the plaintive sound of the Gaelic, the fragrance of the peat-reek drifting from the shore, and the bleat of sheep far up the mountainside that comes faintly to the ear'.

The arrival and departure of these boats became a focal part of the island life, the names and foibles of the captains well known. When a wind of over 8 knots was blowing you knew that if the boat was being skippered by certain men, it would not make shore that day. Others were more intrepid, throwing packages and passengers out in all weathers to waiting ferry boats. An automatic lighthouse was constructed on Castle Island in 1906, one of a chain that stretched down this part of the coast and, in 1911, Thompson built a better pier.

The lack of a deep-water harbour had always made life difficult for the islanders. In 1798 the *Statistical Account* advanced the view that although the Sound made a 'tolerable harbour for a few vessels not exceeding 70 tons, it has no great depth of water, and consequently, with spring tides, such vessels are apt to take the ground, the consequence of which, in severe weather, might be dangerous . . . If a pier, properly planned to afford protection in case of storms, were built here, this harbour might facilitate the navigation of herring buses, both north to the fishing, and south to the market . . . and, if accommodated as above, might prevent buses, when overtaken by contrary winds, or disagreeable weather, from driving back to either and thus be a means of bringing them to their destined port many days earlier.'

Thompson was the architect for the structure of the present pier and it was built under his direction by the islanders. He wanted a pier in water deep enough to take coal vessels weighing up to 300 tons, and his motor ferry. The ferry also made it easier to get goods from the mainland and two shops opened in Cleadale, one owned by the MacLellan family and the other by the MacKays who placed it at one end of their house.

The construction of a new Catholic church was also probably financed by Thompson. This was built in Cleadale in 1910. Before, the priest had lived in Cleadale House, situated just below the present house on the way to the beach, and it incorporated both church and residence. The church was on the upstairs floor, the priest and his housekeeper living downstairs. The old house was knocked down and the stone used to build a wall. The new church and house were connected by a passage and Thompson presented a painting which he thought was by Zurbaran, the 17th-century Spanish artist of religious subjects. The painting was later identified as being of the 16th or 17th-century Italian school but this would probably have hardly mattered to Thompson because, the theory is, the gift was to further assuage the guilt he felt over his earlier desecration of the convent in South America.

Thompson took a morbid interest in his own death. He kept a coffin standing up in a corner of the 'curio room' for years before he died. It was made on the island of solid oak with a lead lining. The man who was soldering the lead had taken 'a good dram' and 'was in good form' and, hammering hard, announced irreverently, 'It won't be easy for him to get out of that'. Thompson does not give the impression that this was his immediate intention. He also chose his grave site with care. In 1913, old and sick, he ordered it to be dug at the south end of Castle Island within view of his three estates, Eigg, Muck and Strathaird. He lay in his bed at Galmisdale and oversaw the work from the window. It took a week. On Christmas Day he was buried. He was placed, it is said, with his head towards Strathaird, his feet facing Muck, and Eigg to his side so that when 'he rose again he would be able to see again his three estates that he loved so well'.

The grave stands on a high mound. Steps lead to the top of the stone plinth surrounded by a now rusting iron railing. A granite slab covers the grave inscribed with the words 'In Memory of Robert Lawrence Thompson of Strathaird, Eigg and Muck who died on 22nd December, 1913, aged 72 years'. The endless view from the top of restless sea and slumbering islands makes it seem the grandest grave site in the Western Isles.

Thompson's grave

EIGG AND ITS PROPRIETORS

Lawrence Thompson left his properties to his brother John who spent little time on the islands and let the shooting on Eigg to a Dane, Sir William Petersen. He bought the island in 1917 and installed himself in MacPherson's lodge. Petersen was a self-made man; the son of a grocer who became a substantial ship-owner and 'a bit of a rough character'. He was enormously tall, weighed 21 stone, had an uncertain temper and was a gambler and big spender. His proprietorship of Eigg was punctuated with episodes of misadventure. The first occurred when, shortly before he paid for Eigg, the lodge mysteriously burnt down while Petersen was out on a day's shooting. The suspicion circulated amongst the islanders that this was not entirely an accident as 'with no lodge he got the island cheaper'.

Petersen exemplified the type of Edwardian who, having made an industrial fortune, wanted to convert the profits into something more lasting and romantic. A Highland estate with a baronial shooting lodge and extensive acres on which to stalk, shoot and fish were essential 'scaffolding to the social climber'. An island was something extra; it gave the opportunity to own a steam yacht and a trip for your guests could be turned into an advantageous circumnavigation of your property. Petersen also possessed a touch of megalomania. He regarded himself as a kind of King, a Norseman who had returned to his own country and he treated the islanders as his subjects. When he first arrived, in the position of the new owner of Eigg, he gave elaborate instructions for his reception. A fire was to be lit on the Scurr. All the islanders were to descend to the pier to greet him and some of the children learn semaphore in order that they could signal with flags 'Welcome to your island Sir William'.

The welcome started to go wrong when the boys made a mistake with the semaphore and were ordered to begin again. Then the small boat that was supposed to meet his yacht and transport him to shore was found to be tied up at Clanranald's pier. Since the tide was out it could not be launched. Sir William was asked to wait but, being impatient, he refused and a badly leaking boat was launched from Thompson's pier. Petersen climbed aboard but when he saw the state of the boat he was furious and shouted, 'Why do you take me in a dinghy more like a basket than a boat?' Lacky, the boatman, answered, 'If you had waited, you would have been taken in the right boat', to which Petersen replied, 'If, that's a bad word, if'.

Sports at the school followed his arrival which Petersen viewed from the top of a specially built cairn of stones. At the end he made a declaration to the assembled islanders saying, 'I am not a stranger here, we owned this island hundreds of years ago, and we had it for three hundred years, and I am coming back to my own island'.

Petersen took over an island whose population was declining and whose way of life was changing. The 1st World War had a cataclysmic effect. Many of the men who joined up were killed. The Donnan's Roll of Honour records ten deaths including six MacLellans. In one family three out of four sons were killed. One died on the day he was decorated and another, wounded in no-man's-land, crawled into a crater and was hit by a sniper. The one son who did return 'never did much after that. The old man continued on his own as long as possible. You would see him going up the side of the hill all on his own'. First one shop and then the other closed in Cleadale; unable to get supplies from the mainland during the war and afterwards there were not enough customers. With fewer people, nightly ceilidhs became a thing of the past and by 1925 they had stopped playing the traditional game of shinty on Laig sands. Hugh MacKinnon wrote a lament to the passing era.

Oh I am deep in gloom today:
It is not my good spirits that drive me on.
Oh I am deep in gloom today. (refrain)

I took a turn down to the shore
To try and pass some hours away:
The wind was tearing from the west,
And the sea swelling in green glens.

Passing by Camus Sgiotaig
I was moving as in a dream:
It had so (affected) my thoughts
To be alone on that walk.

Where we used to gather in a band
When we were young without a care –
Full of life, full of joy,
Full of fun, guileless and innocent.

Where we ran and jumped and wrestled,
Where we lay around the banks:
The putting-stone we so often handled
Overgrown with grey lichen among the rushes.

It has fallen asleep among the rank grass
Since no hand comes near it to move it,
And if it only had the power of speech
It could complete the burden of my song.

And it would tell about foolish days,
Days happy and care-free.
It would tell about valiant lads
Who would poise it on their shoulder.

It would be no disgrace to go and listen
To the tale it had to tell –
How they went away wearing tartan
When the Kaiser struck his blow.

And how they went away and did not come back –
The cause of my sadness at this time:
That's what has left me alone here today
That's what has left me feeling deserted.

Petersen was not a man to notice such changes. He had five factors in nine years and a 'hire and fire 'em' attitude to his estate workers. Hugh MacKinnon remembers that 'there was hardly a day's security on the estate. You would go to work in the morning and by the evening you might have got the sack. Poor old Petersen, what a very tempestuous temper'. Duncan MacKay saw him in a more charitable light and recalled that in 1919, when there was terrible 'flu on the island, Petersen told the factor to kill sheep and open his cellars and give the crofters whisky. He also thought that Petersen would have been a good laird if he had had the money; a fact he suffered from as a boy.

Petersen was a keen sportsman and decided to stock the hill lochs with trout. They were carried in three large containers from Loch Leven and then taken by cart up to the Lochan nam Ban Mora, nearly getting bogged down on the way. 'Even so, after such a rough ride, when the trout were tipped out not one was dead'. Perhaps the venture cost too much money because when, towards the end of Petersen's life, he wanted to stock the loch above Laig farm, named the Giant's Footstep from its peculiar shape and credited by legend to a giant on his way from Rhum to Eigg, he offered Duncan MacKay and six other boys, including the shepherd's son, 2d for every trout they caught by damming streams. The boys were about twelve at the time and willingly undertook the task. However, they discovered that the ghillie never checked the amount in their buckets and started lying about

Kildonnan Bay and Poll nam Partan beach

the correct number, padding the bottom with grass. 'One day there was a stranger with the ghillie and he said "How many have you got?" and we said "Forty-eight" and he started counting and got to nineteen and said "Where are the others?" We said, "Oh they are hiding under the grass at the bottom" and he looked and they weren't there. So you see it doesn't pay to lie'. It also did not pay to do business with unreliable landlords because, in the end, they got 300 trout but Petersen never paid them anything. When he died the shepherd went down to the estate office and banged his stick on the ground and demanded the money but 'they said there was nothing down in the books, and we didn't get a penny'.

Whenever Petersen had money it was quickly spent with great extravagance. One expensive folly was the house he began building for himself in 1920 on the site of the present lodge. It was an elaborate affair, bizarrely constructed out of 'chicken wire, plaster and plywood', with a large central tower 45 feet high from which it gained the name on the island of The White Tower. Using the same method, Petersen built a house for his factor, Garden Cottage, which still stands above the lodge. However, the building material was not suitable for a large structure and the frame of The White Tower started to buckle and bend. The contractors were told their work was not good enough and they should start again. They refused and sued for their money. In 1924, one night when Petersen was off the island this

Cleadale from summit of Ben Tighe

house also went up in flames. The housekeeper was there but when she went to turn on the fire hose there was no water. Later six half-burnt, empty petrol cans were discovered on the shore. They had been thrown into the sea behind the pier but floated back to land for all to see, except the insurance company, who paid up. The fire took four days to burn and the school-children were paraded past the ashes.

Petersen also held large shooting parties and liked to entertain in style, squandering money in the process. When the tenant of Laig Farm left he absorbed this into the estate and kept both houses going, staying at either according to where he pitched up in the evening. He kept a big steam yacht on which he sailed round the islands and one day picked up a traveller and invited him back for dinner. When they arrived at the lodge they were met by the butler who announced 'Dinner is served Sir, here and at Laig'. Petersen was married and had three daughters who were also big spenders and loved racing. They installed an ex-Derby winner in Eigg and used to ride it round the island. It was kept down at Kildonnan and was once borrowed by a crofter to his regret. The horse took off and 'he found himself down the road to Cuagach and over three or four gates within ten minutes and in bed for a week afterwards'.

The spending habits of his daughters, combined with his own expensive tastes, dragged Petersen into ever deeper financial trouble. In spite of this he continued to entertain lavish shooting parties. One of his visitors was the shipping magnate, Sir Walter Runciman. He fell in love with Eigg and used to joke that he hoped Petersen would go bankrupt and then he could 'pick up the island for a song'. In the event Petersen died first, but financial pressures were to

blame. He had gone to Canada in 1925 to try and finalise a deal giving him the rights to transport mail across the Atlantic. His financial backers then reneged on their commitment and the contract was cancelled. The shock killed Petersen

Mary Campbell with her old house in the distance

but, flamboyant to the last, he was returned for burial on Eigg, embalmed and reposing in a brass coffin with a glass top. He was laid in state and all the school-children were taken to have a look by their teacher. 'He was very beautiful,' remembers Mary Campbell, resplendent in full evening dress with a gold chain across his chest. One of the islanders irreverently remarked, 'I wonder if there is a gold watch on the end of that chain'. They never knew. Petersen was buried at Kildonnan; the coffin was so heavy it had to be winched into the grave. He lies there beside his wife, who died in 1919, and one of his daughters, Fiona, who predeceased him in 1920, but you have to fight your way through the undergrowth to find the grave.

Shortly afterwards Sir Walter Runciman bought Eigg from Petersen's executors for £15,000. They were only too glad to get a buyer. Sir Walter's ownership heralded a more orthodox era. His money was solidly grounded in shipping and prodigious amounts were spent on Eigg. The fortune was established by Sir Walter's father. At the age of twelve he ran away from the Border farm where he was raised and became a cabin boy. He started to study, obtained his Master Mariner's Certificate and then, basing himself in South Shields and with a loan from a bank, began buying ships but over-stretched himself. Hearing that the loan was about to be foreclosed, instead of selling, he bought another ship, sold this and then began building vessels. The first was a steam ship called the *Moonlight*. It was completed in 1889 and founded the Moor Line. In 1906 Walter was given a baronetcy and, in 1933, created a baron. He wrote a book about his experiences called *Before the Mast and Aft* and according to Duncan MacKay remained a rough-looking man. 'When we first saw him he had a big beard. A real tramp

he looked'. After Sir Walter acquired Eigg his father came for a visit and thought the island so beautiful he presented him with a cheque for the whole purchase price. Generous gestures were a family characteristic. Sir Walter commuted the annual feu of £5.00, due to the Clanranald, to £500 much to the latter's pleasure.

Sir Walter was born in 1870, educated at Eton and Trinity College, Cambridge, and then joined the family business. In 1891 he became a Liberal MP, rising to be President of the Board of Education and later of Agriculture. He made many improvements to the farms and cottages on Eigg. Robert Atkinson, who visited Eigg in July 1937, wrote in his book *Island Going* that the cultivated parts of the island looked like 'a model farm, with the neat richness of white-washed and freshly painted cottages, fuchsia bushes, small gardens and stone paving. At Cleadale the crofts were a patchwork of potatoes and oats and hay'. The shepherd, Duncan Fergusson, was sent to be educated at agricultural college in Glasgow. He had never left the island and was so frightened his mother and sister had to go with him for company. He found the outside world quite strange and in his first letter home, wrote that he had seen a 'man with a black face and black hands and they say he is black all over'.

Sir Walter was chiefly interested in the island for its sport and, to this end, between three and four thousand pheasants were reared every year. Duncan MacKay recalls that 'He used to come here with shooting parties at Christmas and New Year and everyone on the island was out beating. It was a great shoot.' The Runcimans did not confine their attentions to the pheasants but bagged woodcock, of which there was a great influx in winter, snipe, mallard, the occasional grouse and some of the extensive rabbit population.

Large parties of guests were entertained. Duncan MacKay says 'They were big parties and it was Lord this and Lord that who was staying'. Sir Walter was ably assisted in his position of host by his wife. By all accounts she was a formidable woman who is said to have written a paper which contributed to the downfall of the Liberal party. She used to swim in all weathers from the Cowrie beach, changing in a hut whose dilapidated remains still stand above the shore and is known as Lady Runciman's Bathing Hut. 'It was not just her,' recalls her son, Sir Steven, 'it was that generation. They were very tough. We children never swam.' Lady Runciman also believed in the benefit of fresh air and liked to sit in a draught, even at the end of her life when suffering from rheumatism.

The Runcimans kept a large yacht. It was too large to come inshore and they planned a new pier in deeper water on the adjacent, southern promontory, built in the old way by sinking a boat full of concrete to give a base. However, after making many measurements and calculations, it was decided that the water was too deep and the currents too strong.

Landing on Eigg was quite an occasion. Robert Atkinson says that 'a motor boat came out to meet the steamer' and at the pier there was a lorry waiting on the jetty with 'the laird's title emblazoned upon it, Sir Walter Runciman of Eigg'. The pier was further embellished in 1930 by the addition of some crenellated buildings to house the estate office. The Runcimans also built themselves a new lodge.

When they first arrived their base was Galmisdale House. They added a splendidly ornate bathroom and a kitchen which had the hitherto unknown luxury of hot and cold running water. The house is said to be haunted, children have been heard playing on the stairs and Sir Steven claims they destroyed one ghost. One of the bedrooms was divided into two by a partition and the larger half contained a single bed. People sleeping in the room reported waking to see an old man standing at the foot of the bed but that he was very benign and not frightening. The Runcimans removed the partition to make the room bigger and the old man was never seen again.

The new lodge was designed by a Newcastle architect, Balfour Paul, but with the Runcimans 'looking over his shoulder'. People tried to persuade them to employ Lorimer, the fashionable architect of the day, but Sir Walter would not have him. 'Think what it would have looked like', says Sir Steven, Sir Walter's youngest son, 'another Scottish baronial house'. The lodge, begun in 1925 and completed in 1927, was built by outside contractors. All the materials were transported to Eigg and carried up in carts by the crofters. Three men worked for days loading all the stones into horse-drawn carts. Their hands became skinned with the effort of handling every stone and they were given leather gloves but went through these as well. Originally the whole lodge had a flat roof but Sir Steven disliked it and eventually persuaded his father to put a pitched roof over the central bay. It looked better and prevented some of the problems of damp created by the flat roof; a problem that still bedevils this charming Italianate, ochre-coloured, harled building. It is long and narrow, has a two-storey central recessed columned porch and balcony, flanked by one-storey wings fenced by parapets and decorated with corner urn finials and is now listed as a Grade B building. There are twelve bedrooms, an elegant drawing room and a dining-room placed so that Sir Walter could sit at the top of the table and see the Scurr through the facing window. Sir Steven was put in charge of furnishing the lodge which he did with antique furniture, paintings and chandeliers lit by a 4 kw d.c. hydro-electric plant turned by the burn that gushes through the woods at the back.

Sir Steven also designed the garden, heavily influenced by the one at Inverewe. He was helped by the fact that previous owners had already planted good shelter belts of trees and a micro-climate created by the protective presence of the Scurr rock. There was no fixed plan but whenever Sir Steven saw a plant he liked he would try it and, in the process, achieved a semi-tropical paradise of plants normally more associated with the Scilly Isles, or the South of France, than an island on the same latitude as Labrador. In the acid soil, ferti-lised by seaweed, grow Chilean flame trees, Euchryphia Nymanensis, Enkainthus Campanu-latus, Embrothrium Coccineum, many Mag-nolias and Olearias, Cotoneaster and Strawberry trees and a Eucalyptus. To give the plants further protection he packed them close together; too close for them to develop their full potential but 'if you look at Inverewe they are packed together there. It is like a jungle, you long to push them apart, but it does make it possible for them to flourish'. Sir Walter wanted the drive lined with palms, and Dragon's Blood ones were planted. At its side there is a vegetable garden and by the gate a rose garden, small orchard and tennis court. The whole garden was tended until his retirement by Donald Campbell. Its lushness contrasts with the wildness of the rest of the island. The sea can only be glimpsed through a gap in the trees, the wind softly soughs through their tops and the sharpest

The pier

The Lodge

146

sounds are those of a waterfall and the many song birds.

In 1931, when the National Government was formed, Sir Walter was summoned from Eigg by radio to be President of the Board of Trade and, in 1937, Chamberlain made him a Viscount. Sir Walter is chiefly remembered for his unsuccessful attempt to mediate between the Sudetan Germans and the Czech Government at the start of the 2nd World War. The mission was destined to fail and Sir Walter only undertook the task after a personal plea from George VI. The effort, and the feeling of responsibility for its consequences, had a lasting effect. At the beginning of the war he developed Parkinson's disease and was forced to resign from office. From then on he seldom visited Eigg and died in 1949.

The island was left jointly to his two sons, Steven and Walter. The youngest, Steven, inherited the lodge and came to regard the house as his country home, staying for at least a month at intervals throughout the year; in January and February, May and June and again in September and October. It suited his work. By this time he was in his forties, a man of immense erudition and charm, and a distinguished academic: a lecturer at Cambridge and other universities, historian and writer specialising in the Byzantine period. Many of his books were drafted on Eigg including *A History of the Crusades* which has become a classic. Sir Steven used to arrive with a suitcase of books and a suitcase of groceries and settle down to work in the long evenings. It was said he so hated to be disturbed that 'people who telephoned never tried twice'. His main disruption was his father who he believes haunts the lodge. Sir Walter never used the front door but came in through a side one leading into the boot-room. When Sir Steven was sitting alone working in the next door study he used to hear his footsteps coming in through that door and walking into the house.

Another ghost appears at the back door, 'a big huge fellow'. He was seen by Duncan MacKay's mother who worked as cook at the lodge. One day she went to the back door and 'there was a man standing there, as big as the shepherd. She didn't believe it but it was there'. When Sir Steven became sole owner he reduced the staff to one, Donald Campbell's mother. She became rather old and unable to see much so the lodge was never very clean. He longed for one of her sons to marry a 'nice young girl and he could then employ her', but Mrs Campbell ruled her sons with a 'rod of iron' and they never dared while she was alive. Sir Steven did his own cooking and was a keen jam-maker. The islanders were much amused by the fact that, every year in September, he was to be seen 'picking brambles for making jams and jellies'. He also did his own shopping, walking to the shop with a wicker basket over his arm. The islanders regarded him as a 'great scholar' and were of the opinion that 'no ordinary person could read his books'. The gamekeeper took one out of the library but said 'it is taking me all my time to read it, every word was needing to be looked up in a dictionary. Only professionals could read it'.

Sir Steven was extremely interested in music and installed a Bechstein grand piano in the drawing-room. It was tuned by a man who came on a 'busman's holiday round the islands every year'. From the Bechstein on Eigg he moved to another on Canna and a Steinway grand on Rhum. Sir Steven played himself and so did many of his wide circle of friends who included Yehudi Menuhin and Sir Arthur Bliss. He found that seeing people on the island often showed up their characters; it pushed them to their edges and exposed any deficiencies. A famous historian's wife came and never admired a thing, 'And it was not as though the weather was awful and drizzling but beautiful and everything looked wonderful. How could she be so insensitive'. Whereas the Greek ambassador was totally enthusiastic and amazed by Eigg saying, 'How wonderful, why this is more beautiful than Greece, but the sea is less warm'.

Art is another subject on which Sir Steven was deeply knowledgeable. He doubted that the painting Thompson had given to the Cleadale church was by Zurbaran and saw that it was suffering badly from damp. He had it removed and sent for restoration and identification. The experts pronounced that it was of the 16th or 17th century Italian School and, to prevent it being damaged again, it was decided not to return the painting to Eigg. The Runcimans wanted it to be put in the Kelvinside Galleries in Glasgow, with a notice saying 'lent by the islanders of Eigg' because Glasgow is where they all go and have relations. This wish was over-ruled by the Bishop and the painting now hangs in the Catholic church in Oban.

A party for the islanders used to be given annually at Christmas and Easter. The Runcimans built the present timber ceilidh hall for the purpose. From then on it became the main island gathering place where ceilidhs, weddings and other large functions are held.

A notable islander at this time was Archie MacDonald who was the estate boatman. He had a long black beard and was immensely strong, regularly rowing to Arisaig and back in a day. His home was Pier Cottage and here he kept a pet otter, Tibby. She followed him like a dog and

caught fish in the bay. At the end of his life Archie became crippled with arthritis, had to use crutches to move and make an increasing number of visits to the hospital. He became worried about Tibby's future and decided to give her to Gavin Maxwell at Camusfearna. This was not a success as Maxwell describes in *Raven Seek Thy Brother*. The otter was kept confined in an enclosure but managed to escape and, uncannily, headed northeast in the direction in which Archie had left unseen by her several weeks before. She was found in the village and returned to Camusfearna. Her cage was made even more secure but Tibby repeatedly escaped. Eventually, obviously making up her mind she would not be caught again, she located a man in the village who most resembled her master, in that he was a cripple on crutches. She tried to attach herself to him, carrying grass and beginning to build a nest under his

house. The man was not otter minded and, repulsed, Tibby left the area. Months later Maxwell received a telephone call from a 'slightly inebriated gentleman' who said he had a female otter for sale. Maxwell became convinced it was Tibby and after some negotiations offered him £8.00 to release the otter. The deal came to nothing as Tibby then disappeared. The next telephone call was from a man who had been followed to his house by an otter. 'Acting on a sudden inspiration,' Maxwell asked, 'you don't by any chance use crutches, do you?' 'Yes,' he replied, with astonishment in his voice, 'but how in the world could you know that?' Maxwell told him the story and the man promised to telephone again if she came back but 'I never heard from him again'.

Sir Steven's elder brother, Walter, succeeded their father, becoming 2nd Viscount of Doxford. He was more often called by his second name of

Leslie and had many maritime interests which embraced being director of the family shipping line now named Walter Runciman & Co. Ltd. He enjoyed yachting more than shooting but used to take the lodge in August and entertain shooting parties. Sir Steven disliked shooting and discouraged his brother and he gradually stopped. Then the gamekeeper died and was not replaced and the pheasants became 'as tame as hens'. Walter was first married to the writer, Beatrice Lehmann, and then to an American, Katherine Schuyler of New York. His eldest son, also called Walter but known as Gary, married a South African girl who was not amused by Eigg. According to Duncan MacKay she announced that 'When we go on holiday we want to follow the sun' and on Eigg when they came 'it was usually drizzling and raining so it wasn't suiting them'.

Gary's lack of enthusiasm made his father keen to sell Eigg, but Sir Steven steadfastly resisted the proposal. However, he began to get old and found the journey a strain. He also wanted to leave London and felt that Eigg was a long way for visiting friends. His huge library – which now fills three rooms and contains books in eight languages – would have been difficult to house and might have become affected by the damp. Eventually, in 1966, he decided the island would

have to be sold and one Thursday morning wrote to his brother in time to catch that day's post. The incoming mail brought a copy of *Country Life* and in it was a bad picture of his present house in the Borders. 'It must have been fate,' says Sir Steven.

The island was advertised for sale as 'A perfectly secluded island of the Old World, the very beautiful island of Eigg'. It was bought by Captain Robert Evans, a Shropshire landowner and farmer, for £82,000. He promised to endeavour to make Eigg, what the Runcimans felt it could be, 'a profitable thing for somebody prepared to live there all the time'. It was not like 'some of the small islands that exist only as rich men's toys'. During the Runcimans' time the farming, at its best, never did more than break even and normally ran at a loss.

The 2nd World War was another watershed in the life of the island. Recruitment took more men away and many never returned. Fewer people meant less social life and more were attracted to the mainland, especially the young. The desire and energy to continue with the hard, old, traditional crofting way of life among those who remained diminished. The general cultivation of oats, potatoes and hay was neglected. Fewer cattle were kept and the drovers stopped their

annual visits. The decline was obvious in 1955 when F. Fraser Darling wrote in his *West Highland Survey* that 'This basalt island is one of high potential fertility which has been allowed to go almost to dereliction . . . most of the Eigg crofters are now elderly and the future of the island as a crofting community is precarious . . . bracken is all too prevalent . . . the construction of a proper harbour would make it reasonably possible for the high potential of this favoured island to be reached. Without it, there is no hope'.

Robert Evans wanted to develop the farming in tune with the sensitivity of Eigg's unique community but, in fact, seldom visited the place due to poor health and personal troubles. Duncan MacKay remembers him as 'a fine man but a bit on the old side. He went down to Grulin and sat down by the side of the road and could hardly get up'. By 1971 Eigg was on the market again. It was sold for a handsome profit. Evans justified accusations of using the island for property speculation by saying he was not capitalising on the deal because he had spent so much money while he was there and was merely trying to get some back.

Eigg attracted the attention of Bernard Farnhum-Smith, who paid £120,000 for its charms. He farmed in Sussex and ran the Anglyn Trust, a school for mentally handicapped children. A similar establishment was planned for Eigg and Farnhum-Smith also aimed to develop the agriculture and make the community more self-sufficient by running a boat service, building an abattoir and opening up the island for tourists. None of his ideas reached fruition. During his three-year tenure he kept his house in Sussex, returning there from October to April, never had more than three handicapped boys on Eigg and, at the end, none. The translation from Sussex farmer to Hebridean laird proved beyond his financial and mental resources.

The lack of a laird with limitless money meant that people who were just making a living before became very hard up. More people left and life for those who remained became increasingly lonely. There were just not the people for 'big get togethers'. Eigg could not withstand further depopulation and by 1975 Farnhum-Smith's policies made the islanders fearful for their survival. The population was down to thirty-nine and there were only two children in the school. A plea for help was made to the Highlands and Islands Development Board. They decided to step in and buy the island but, in the event, their offering price was topped by one of £250,000. It was advanced by Keith Schellenberg and, in 1976, he became the new proprietor of Eigg. Bernard Farnhum-Smith left for the last time and, as he sailed away, an islander muttered incantations and curses over the water.

THE ISLAND TODAY

Keith Schellenberg, a passionate individualist and sportsman, was born in Yorkshire in 1930. His family originated in Liechtenstein but, finding themselves on the wrong side of an 18th-century European war, they moved to England and began farming in Nottinghamshire. Business was more to the taste of Schellenberg's grandfather and he began several industrial companies in Yorkshire, a line continued by his son and grandson. Property in Aberdeenshire, owned by Schellenberg's second wife, the Hon. Margaret Udny Hamilton, introduced him to Scotland. They divorced in 1980 and he is now married to Suki, the third daughter of

Major-General R. E. Urquhart, who commanded the famous and fatal battle of Arnhem in 1944. She was also married before and between them the Schellenbergs have eight children, seven girls and a boy.

Business is not Schellenberg's only link with Yorkshire; he also captained the county at Rugby; one sporting success in a range which includes being a member of the 1956 and 1964 British Olympic bobsleigh teams, racing antique Bentleys and power-boats. Sailing is another of his pursuits and through it the Hebrides became one of his loves. Yachting round the islands made him want to own one. He considered Gigha when it came on the market, but then saw Eigg in 1975 and decided that this was the island for him. 'It was more savage and the topography was more varied.'

He decided that resuscitating the island would be a challenge for his middle years and made high, idealistic plans for stabilising its dwindling society and improving its economy while maintaining the unspoilt Hebridean atmosphere. Schellenberg is a vegetarian and keen conservationist and immediately declared the whole island a nature reserve, forbade shooting and only allows a limited amount of fishing. Seven areas of Eigg have now been designated sites of Special Scientific Interest and the Scottish Wildlife Trust keeps three reserves.

The estate now amounts to 5,000 acres and incorporates all the farms on the south end of the island: Grulin, Galmisdale, Kildonnan, Sandavore and Sandaveg. Most of the land has reverted to rough grazing or moorland and there are only 100 acres of arable on which hay is grown. Recently 400 acres of unproductive moorland below the Scurr ridge have been planted with forestry. Sheep are the main enterprise and at present they run 2,000 Blackface and Cheviot ewes. The numbers of cattle have been reduced to about forty cross-bred and Luig cows which, although slow-maturing, are largely self-sufficient. Cattle are better for the land and help check the all-pervading spread of bracken but require expensive labour, and storms and the public ferry service make taking them to market, at Oban or Fort William, a nightmare. The latter can mean that cattle which should be sold in August eventually reach the market in early December when the price has fallen and valuable reserves of winter feed consumed.

The island has been opened up for tourists. Schellenberg thinks that Eigg is such a lovely place others should enjoy it as well and that it is necessary for people 'working under oppressive urban conditions to have a place where they can restore their fundamental values'. About 4,000 people a year take advantage of these facilities. They come as passing yachtsmen, day visitors, families wanting to rent one of his holiday cottages – most of which are restored crofts – or to stay in the guest house at Kildonnan. Visitors often find themselves drawn into a team game. Schellenberg pursues his sporting interests on Eigg and whenever he 'gets a nice group of campers, or anyone else, we try to get something going like football, cricket or hockey'. These sports also form part of the Eigg Games held every August. Several teams compete, over three

days, in a multifarious range of events often with more bravado than expertise. There are genteel garden sports – croquet, petanque and badminton; spartan water sports – swimming, sailing and wind-surfing; every form of running race including a marathon, and finally a war game between the Hanoverians and Jacobites, the latter team led by the Clanranalds mounting a comeback in their traditional territory.

On the estate six full-time people are employed and wherever possible people living on the island are given the jobs. In the summer up to fifteen more help with the tourists. Some of these are outsiders and they often fall under the spell of Eigg, keep returning and a few end up living on the island.

Schellenberg's attitude to incomers has changed. At first, anxious to build up the population num-

bers, he encouraged anyone. Then he realised they were attracting the wrong type of person 'wandering itinerants who found the island a nice refuge but were not mentally strong enough to cope with the life and earn a living in the environment. It is very important to have people with the resources to take the difficulties and isolation and who have a strong outside base to which they can return and keep in touch'.

Half of Eigg's fluctuating population of sixty-five are now incomers. There are more indigenous islanders living in and around Fort William than on the island. The incomers arrive in odd ways and for various reasons. The story of how Pat Campbell ended up on Eigg provides a nice illustration. She was divorced, fed up with her good job in London as an editor for a commercial publisher, and felt her life was in a rut. Reading the *Lady* magazine over lunch one day she saw an advertisement for a house-keeper on an island she did not even know existed and decided to apply for the post. There was no reply but, three months later, while she was in the bath the telephone rang. It was Suki Schellenberg asking her to come for an interview. Pat went, immediately felt Eigg was right for her, and accepted the job. Returning to London, within one day she gave in her notice, sold her car and rented her house. The last words on the advertisement were 'Friendly gardener' put in by Schellenberg to indicate that the job would not be totally isolated. Within six months

Pat had married the gardener, Donald Campbell. In Pat's wake came her daughter and son-in-law, Trevor. They first made visits, which got longer and eventually they settled on Eigg. Trevor makes baskets and works for the estate.

Five years is the average length of stay for incomers who cannot adapt to the life. As one said, 'the society does get a bit small and limited. In the summer it is not so bad with all the holiday visitors but in winter there is nothing to talk about but each other. Everyone knows exactly what you are doing. There is more privacy in the centre of London than on Eigg'. If you are going

The shop and post office

to survive you have to join in as 'it is really one large family and if you don't become part of the community there is no life'. Pat Campbell admits that she might have left if she had not married Donald. Even now she occasionally feels the need of some culture and goes south but soon wants to return. 'Eigg is a place you either love or hate, there is no in-between. You can't feel half-hearted about it. Life is much more basic but means more as well. In the south it is all geared up to commercialism, here it is much more simple. I admire Donald because he can survive without any of the things other people seem to need. But I couldn't survive without him, just in a practical way like bringing in the coal, keeping the water going and all the other things that make up life here.

'You feel part of a family here which is why you have got to fit in and be accepted. It is such a close-knit community, much more so than even a village. Events like funerals are far more moving.

Whoever dies you go to their funeral. I have been to more here than in the whole of my life. In London that wouldn't happen. Everybody goes to the weddings as well. We had the best wedding in the world. Everybody was involved. All the food was made on Eigg. Nothing swish, just simple food, everyone cooks a dish. We got married in the church and then went to the ceilidh hall for the reception and everyone was so happy.'

Most of the incomers are young and the islanders admit they would rather have them than nobody. 'They are not all bad, just different. They help us and each other', and introduce innovations like TVs and videos. Musicians join the Eigg band that plays at ceilidhs. Major ceilidhs take place every fortnight throughout the summer and at the main festivals such as New Year. Small ones frequently take place, as they always have, in people's houses but the talk is more neighbourly gossip than the old stories. The Queen's Silver Jubilee was marked

The Ceilidh Hall

156

by a bonfire on the Scurr, part of the chain that stretched the length of Britain.

Crofting land amounts to 1,500 acres around Cleadale and is exempt from the freehold of the estate. Many have been amalgamated into units of about 14 acres on which the existing dozen crofters keep cross-bred cattle, about thirty in all. A bull is shared with the estate, funded by the government and changed every two years. They also keep a few sheep and grow crops, mainly hay and oats. None are self-sufficient and rely on stores from the mainland to maintain daily life. Few grow vegetables and sliced bread and long-life milk have supplanted home baking and the household cow. Most of the houses now have electricity, fired by their own generators and powered by the burns which also provide their running water supply. A bewildering array of hose pipes snake their way from burns to nearby houses and the night pulsates with the throbbing of generators.

Crofting is still not a full-time occupation and, in true tradition, most practise other trades and some several; like a small company performing a play with many parts, the same people keep appearing in different roles and guises. Angus Kirk helps with the ferry and, with his wife Marie, runs the shop and post office, a white-painted corrugated iron hut, still situated where Thompson placed them, in the centre of the island. Supplies come from Edinburgh, Glasgow and Fort William. Transport costs are high and, since there is no electricity or water on the premises, stock is necessarily limited. They avoid fresh meat and perishable vegetables but do have unexpected extras like garlic. Whenever Marie goes to Glasgow she looks in the shops for things that might go on Eigg. Dougie Campbell delivers the three posts a week on his bicycle. The work takes about ten hours but more if there is an adverse wind.

The shop is a great gathering place, as is the pier. Here there is a tearoom run by Marie, the wife of Colin Carr, who is farm manager to the

estate. There is a craft shop on the pier stocked by Suki Schellenberg with choice Hebridean products, pictures and books. The pier also provides the base for any commercial fishing done on Eigg. Two fishermen catch mostly shellfish which has become big business. Lobster, prawn, some scallops, limpets and velvet crabs end up in Spain and there are plans for squid to join them. The arrival of the ferry boats is a major event for the islanders. As a boat appears on the horizon the island empties as everybody converges on the pier to collect the goods they have ordered from the mainland, exchange news and views and share a dram.

MacBraynes operate the official, government-subsidised ferry and its high transport costs and wayward timetable that appears to take little account of passengers' convenience are the cause of much complaint. Murdo Grant fills an important gap, running a daily ferry service from Arisaig in his boat the *Shearwater*, during the summer months. Even so, many feel strongly that a change in the system would aid the island's economy.

The crofters' cattle are transported to the mainland by MacBraynes. This job is overseen by Angus MacKinnon. He gathers the cattle together, takes them to the mainland and sells them at market, in his capacity of Clerk of the Township. MacKinnon also represents the crofters' interests in other ways and is their spokesman at the Crofters' Commission. His duties include being Special Police Constable. This is not an arduous job, crime in Eigg is virtually non-existent and few doors have locks. Arrests take time as the official policeman has to come from Mallaig. The only trouble recently was created by outsiders. Some members of a party of under-privileged children from Glasgow broke into the post office and stole money. The event made the newspapers because the next day a party of MPs happened to be visiting the island and, while on a guided tour, stopped on a hill only to see £50 worth of notes blowing around.

Angus MacKinnon is also the designated road mender under contract to the Highland Region. The road stretches 4½ miles from Howlin to the pier and 1½ miles down the steep brae to Kildonnan. Angus says that 'The wet causes awful damage, but you just have to fill the pot holes in as best you can. There is terrible trouble getting materials. By the time you have finished it is time to start again. All the road was used for was horses and carts. It was not built for heavy traffic so it goes to pieces very easily.' The road was tarmaced in 1959 although the first car arrived in 1921. Today there are more rusting by the roadside than there are on the road. Many have been there so long they are intertwined with undergrowth. A few years ago there was a rumour that a crusher was going to tour the island but sadly it has yet to arrive. No one brings new cars to Eigg as the salt air, rough roads and rudimentary maintenance all take their toll. It is a constant source of wonderment to the visitor how many of these operate with doors, windows, headlights and many of the other accoutrements normally considered essential, all missing. The doctor gets a free car and his is the smartest on the island. His mileage is slight and the car only needs servicing every four years.

Hector MacLean has been the doctor on Eigg since 1951. He also plays the pipes, used to keep bees, and is a notable figure in Eigg, his stocky frame invariably encased in a kilt. He says the most common ailment is the Eigg bug. It is particularly prevalent in spring, takes the form of acute diarrhoea and vomiting and goes almost as quickly as it comes. They get the same on oil rigs. People on Eigg call it The Bomb. 'Today you never know with diseases, something can start in Sydney, Australia, and be on Eigg five days later.' Another common complaint is depression, suffered by both incomers and islanders. The former get it because 'many arrive on impulse and are not prepared for the isolated life' and the latter since the population declined. 'Old people remember the days when there was lots of fun on the island, lots of people, they have long memories and now get depressed.' Even so people live long lives on Eigg and in his time there have been two centenarians. In cases of serious illness the doctor can summon the lifeboat from Mallaig and in a 'life or death' situation an RAF helicopter from Lossiemouth or Kinloss. 'Even so it is desirable that any islander developing a serious illness should do so in reasonable weather.' He visits the other islands

Dottie Campbell, postman; Hector MacLean, doctor; Angus Kirk, shopkeeper

Lackie Maclean, lobster fisherman; Mary Bell MacDonald outside her croft; Dolly Ferguson, widow of Duncan; George Carr; Morag MacKinnon

as and when required. The weather makes regular visits impossible but he tries to go about every three weeks.

A dentist visits Eigg twice a year under NHS regulations. An elaborate chair and equipment await his visits, installed in a large new surgery. It was begun in 1978 by workmen flown in by helicopter, but their start was delayed because they forgot to bring any tools with them. The building cost £100,000 and is an example of bureaucratic folly. MacLean says, 'It is not necessary to have such a large building but the authorities in Aberdeen, who have never been here, could not envisage a smaller one. I regard this as the King of Spain would regard the present of a white elephant'.

The doctor has a computer, and the school two television sets for school broadcasts. Outside there is an enormous aerial christened 'Jodrell Bank'. The school, a handsome grey stone building with a playground to one side, is situated in the centre of the island. At present there are seven children being taught by one teacher. They are brought by school bus, a land-rover driven by Dugal MacKinnon, and even the youngest does a full day. Small classes mean the children get individual attention and often do well. What they lack is the competition of larger classes and mixed social contacts.

They get this when, at the age of twelve, they transfer to the Secondary School in Fort William. The disadvantage of this arrangement is that they

Island children

have to live in a hostel and are not supervised at weekends. For twelve-year-olds, whose knowledge of the world is limited to Eigg, who have never caught a bus or seen traffic, it can be dangerous. This unhappy arrangement has caused many families to leave the island.

Few of the children speak Gaelic now. Angus MacKinnon says that he is really bi-lingual. 'I curse in Gaelic and I think in Gaelic and English.' When the islanders are together they speak Gaelic but when outnumbered by incomers, English. The children are not taught it in school and 'unless they have a Gaelic-speaking parent they don't learn it and so it dies out. When I went to school there were very few entirely English-speaking people. We were taught in English but we spoke Gaelic amongst ourselves out in the playground'.

Until 1950 the minister was required to speak Gaelic. Then, as a reflection of the declining numbers of Gaelic speakers and the difficulties of getting ministers to serve such remote parishes, it became 'desirable' rather than 'essential' for him to know the language. The Church of Scotland minister is now based in Mallaig. His parish covers an area of 594 square miles and, as a result, he visits Eigg only once a month. Church services happen on any day of the week and are usually in the evenings. People of all denominations attend. The Roman Catholic church is now linked with Knoydart and the priest comes every fortnight, taking services in the church at Cleadale. It is also patronised by people of both faiths but mainly by the old Catholic families, MacKinnons, Kirks and Campbells. Outside, sheepdogs sprawl round the entrance and the sound of the sea breaking in Laig strand mingles with the hymns sung unaccompanied by an organ. A spirit pervading the service shows the intensely religious feeling still existing on Eigg.

The church is lit by gas-lights and is much in need of repair. Many of the windows have panes missing. Its state is in stark contrast to the brand new lighthouse and huge telephone exchange; both donated by a Government whose behaviour often resembles that of a profligate parent with an awkward child it tries to avoid. Money is spent in an arbitrary, impractical fashion as if to assuage its guilt. An expensive and unnecessarily large doctor's surgery and telephone exchange are bought and a lighthouse that still works efficiently replaced when what would really help the island is a new ferry boat and better service. Government officials seldom visit and, with few votes to be gained, neither do MPs. Too often it gives with one hand and takes with the other. Idle incomers can live on social security while industrious islanders have been driven out by its policies. Rates are charged but the services are minimal. There is no rubbish collection or mains electricity.

Keith Schellenberg tries to maintain the delicate balance between keeping a viable economy going on the estate, opening Eigg to the public, and conserving the wildlife. 'I am the first to try and run the island as a commercial enterprise but managing an estate on an island is quite different to one on the mainland. The consumer durable society does not work once you get round Ardnamurchan Point. People attack anyone who tries to do something on his own but what is to happen to these islands if they are not to become derelict or owned by State Quangos?'

The population of Eigg is rising and this should continue while there are people who feel the tough, demanding life, lack of modern amenities and of large financial gain are balanced by the beauty of the landscape and a strong sense of community.

Bibliography

Atkinson, Robert, *Island Going*, Glasgow, 1949

Banks, Noel, *Six Inner Hebrides*, Newton Abbot, 1977

Campbell, J. L., *Canna – The Story of a Hebridean Island*, Oxford, 1984

Carmichael, Alexander, *Carmina Gadelica – Hymns and Incantations*, Vol. 1–2, Edinburgh, 1900

Cooper, Derek, *Road to the Isles, Travellers in the Hebrides 1770–1914*, London, 1979

Dunbar, John Telfer, *Herself – The Life and Photographs of M. E. M. Donaldson*, Edinburgh, 1979

Ferguson, Duncan, *The Island of Eigg*, Edinburgh, 1975

Fraser-Darling, F. and Morton Boyd, *Highlands and Islands*, Glasgow, 1969

Glover, Janet R., *The Story of Scotland*, London, 1977

Goodrich-Freer, A., *Outer Isles*, London, 1902

Grant, I. F., *Highland Folkways*, London, 1961

Gregory, Donald, *The History of the Western Highlands and Isles of Scotland from AD 1493 to AD 1625*, 2nd ed., London, 1881

Hall, Rev. James, *Travels in Scotland*, Vol. 1–2, London, 1807

Kennedy-Fraser, Marjorie and Kenneth MacLeod, *Songs of the Hebrides*, Vol. 1–4, London, 1909

MacCulloch, J. A., *The Misty Isles of Skye*, Stirling, 1927

MacDiarmid, Hugh, *The Islands of Scotland*, London, 1939

Macdonald, Donald, J. of Castleton, *Clan Donald*, Edinburgh, 1978

Mackay, James A., *Skye and the Small Isles*, Islands Postal History Series No. 4, Dumfries, 1978

Mackinnon, Hugh, *Summary of Interviews with Donald Archie MacDonald*, Edinburgh, 1973

MacEwan, Lawrence, *A Guide to Eigg and Muck*, Isle of Muck, 1981

MacLean, Charles, *Island on the Edge of the World: the story of St Kilda*, Edinburgh, 1977

Martin, Martin, *Description of the Western Islands of Scotland*, London, 1705

Maxwell, Gavin, *Raven Seek Thy Brother*, London, 1984

Miller, Hugh, *The Cruise of the Betsy*, London, 1858

Munro, Dean Donald, ed. R. W. Munro, *A Description of the Western Isles of Scotland called Hybrides*, c.1549, revised ed., Stirling, 1934

Necker, de Saussure, L. A., *A Voyage to the Hebrides*, Vol. 8, London, 1822

Pennant, Thomas, *A Tour in Scotland and Voyage to the Hebrides, 1774–6*, London, 1772

Robertson, Rev. C. M., 'Topography and Traditions of Eigg', *Transactions of the Gaelic Society of Inverness*, Vol. 22, 1897–98, Inverness, 1900

Schellenberg, Keith, *Holiday Accommodation Guide, 1983–4*, Isle of Eigg, 1984

School of Scottish Studies, *Tocher*, Vols. 10, 36, Edinburgh, 1973

Scottish Development Department, *Area of Inverness, List of Buildings of Architectural or Historic Interest*, Edinburgh, 1965

Scottish Wildlife Trust, *The Isle of Eigg Reserves, Wardens Report*, 1984

Shaw, Frances J., *The Northern and Western Islands of Scotland, their Economy and Society in the Seventeenth Century*, Edinburgh, 1980

Simpson, W. Douglas, *Portrait of Skye and the Outer Hebrides*, London, 1967

Sinclair, Rt. Hon. Sir John, *The Statistical Account of Scotland, Vol. 10, The Western Isles*, Edinburgh, 1791–99

Sinclair, Rt. Hon. Sir John, *Analysis of the Statistical Account of Scotland*, Edinburgh, 1831

Skene, William Forbes, *Celtic Scotland, Vol. 3: The Description of the Isles of Scotland*, Edinburgh, 1876–80

Sutherland, Halliday, *Hebridean Journey*, London, 1939

Swire, Otto, F., *The Inner Hebrides and their Legends*, London, 1964

Thompson, Francis, *The Highlands and Islands*, London, 1974

Trevelyan, G. M., *A Shortened History of England*, Harmondsworth, 1974

Twidell, J. W. and A. A. Pinney, *Energy, Supply and Use on the Small Scottish Island of Eigg – Energy Vol. 10*, Oxford, 1985

Walker, John D. D., *An Economical History of the Hebrides and Highlands of Scotland*, Edinburgh, 1808

Weir, Tom, *Scottish Islands*, Newton Abbot, 1976

Acknowledgements

This book could not have been written without the help of many people. I would like to thank my sister and brother-in-law, Suki and Keith Schellenberg who gave me their wholehearted assistance and encouragement during its writing.

I have relied heavily for much of the latter part of my material on the memory and experiences of the residents of Eigg. I am grateful to all those who talked to me but in particular am indebted to Duncan MacKay. He sat patiently for many hours answering questions into a hated tape-recorder while his sister, Kitty Anne, filled the few gaps in his memory. Angus MacKinnon, the last of a line of traditional bearers of Eigg culture, was also extremely helpful, as were Hector MacLean, Morag Campbell, Donald and Pat Campbell, Mary Campbell, Marie and Angus Kirk, Marie and Colin Carr and Joan Jamieson.

There were others who provided information or helped in special ways. Sir Steven Runciman kindly provided a fund of stories of his family's proprietorship of Eigg. Ranald MacDonald, the hereditary chief of Clanranald, talked with great willingness. Donald Dewar gave me the benefit of his deep knowledge of Scottish history and literature. Elspeth and Menzies Campbell, my elder sister and brother-in-law, lent me their cottage, Calzie, where I began the book, while my parents often had me to stay during its writing. Adam Urquhart, my brother, gave valuable advice. Elaine Hay, secretary to the Isle of Eigg Estate, obliged whenever asked for assistance. David Prichard was a support and did some time-saving photocopying. Eric Ellington tramped the island with me and without his photographs the book would not be nearly as handsome and evocative.